Miller

Betsy –
To the next generation of
philanthropists!
♡ Dr. Holly Mioni

Holly Hull Miori

Millennial Philanthropy

Next Generation Fund Development for Professionals and Nonprofits

Holly Hull Miori
Grapevine, USA

ISBN 978-3-031-30268-8 ISBN 978-3-031-30269-5 (eBook)
https://doi.org/10.1007/978-3-031-30269-5

Cover image: DisobeyArt

This Palgrave Macmillan imprint is published by the registered company Springer Nature Switzerland AG
The registered company address is: Gewerbestrasse 11, 6330 Cham, Switzerland

...It is more blessed to give than to receive.—Acts 20:35

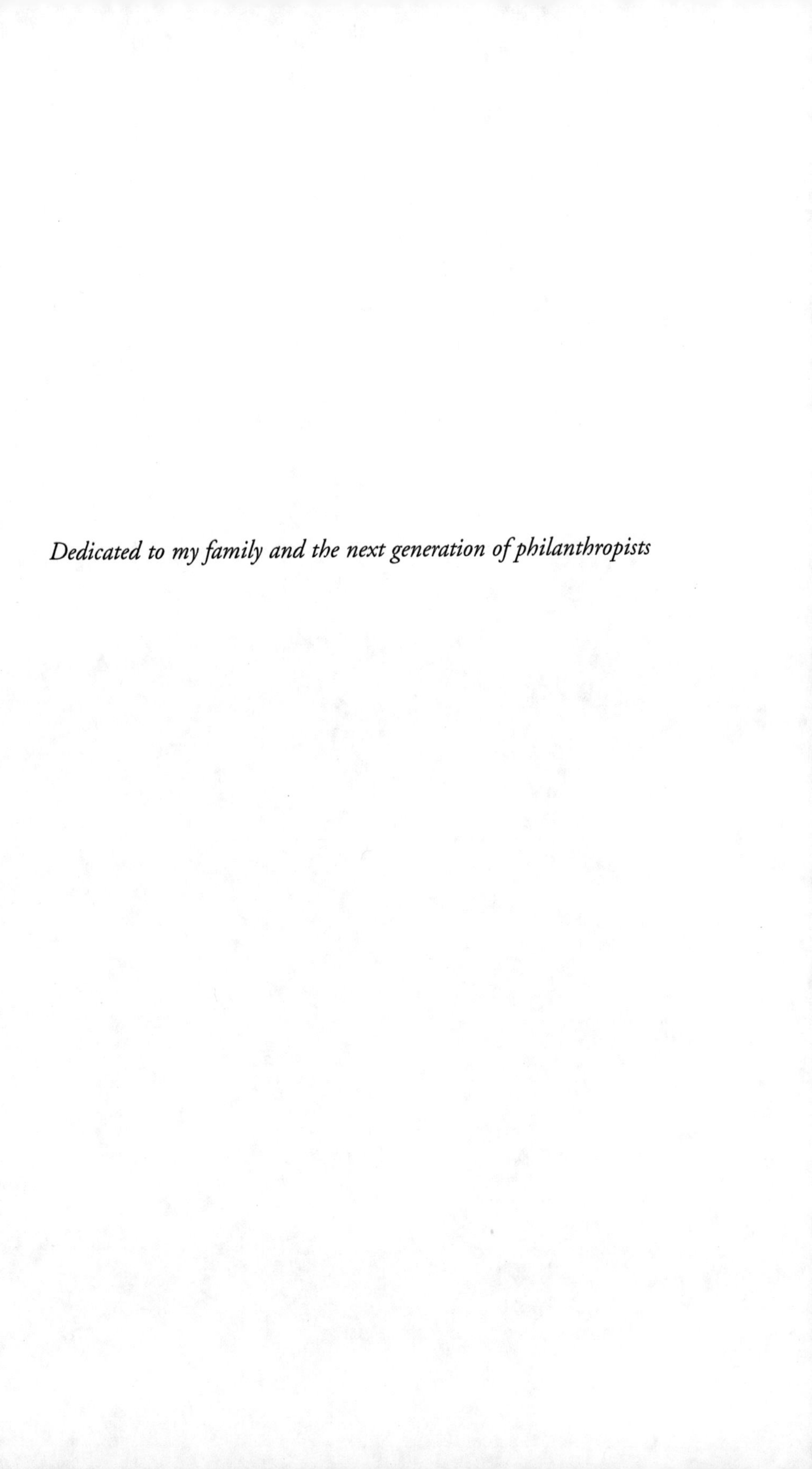

Dedicated to my family and the next generation of philanthropists

Foreword

Holly Miori's book which explores layers of detail related to millennials and their approach to philanthropy. Holly provides a fresh perspective on this emerging topic by drawing on her extensive research in the field. Her insights and recommendations are particularly valuable for anyone interested in with younger generations in the nonprofit sector.

One of the book's strengths is its emphasis on the unique characteristics and preferences of millennials when it comes to giving. Holly's research reveals that millennials prioritize causes that align with their values and are interested in seeing tangible results from their donations. She also emphasizes the importance of transparency and accountability in nonprofit organizations, as well as the need for organizations to embrace technology and social media to engage with this next wave of donors.

Overall, Holly's book is a valuable resource for nonprofit professionals, volunteers, and donors looking to better understand and engage with the millennial generation. Her research-based insights offer practical advice and strategies for organizations seeking to building meaningful relationships with the important demographic and those surrounding it.

Houston, USA

Kevin J. Foyle, MBA, CFRE
Association of Fundraising
Professionals Global Immediate
Past Chair

Acknowledgments

A book journey comes with hard work but with many blessings. While working on my dissertation, my goal was always to fulfill the study into something that would be useful for the academic community and fundraisers. I hope this book meets and exceeds your expectations and conveys my love for celebrating what the nonprofit community can do to engage the next generations.

I am grateful for my circle of friends, family, and academic advisors. A special thank you to my husband Michael and our children Isabelle and Trenton—may our children continue to find inspiration and good in the world. An extra special thank you is due to our extended family for their love and support. I also extend a note of appreciation to the many friends and development colleagues who provided inspiration with their own stories of philanthropy and work in development. I am inspired by you.

As one of my favorite donors used to say, "What's next?," I hope this book tells us what to do with resources. As a development professional, I have had the privilege of meeting so many wonderful donors who entrusted me with their stories. Many of these stories provided the framework for this book, and for that I am grateful. I also wish to note my appreciation for the continued support, patience, and love of the faculty at The University of Texas at Dallas, especially the members of my dissertation committee and faculty and in particular Dr. Meghna Sabharwal, Dr. Elizabeth Searing, and Dr. Allison Russell.

I would also like to send a special thank you to BvB Dallas, GRACE of Grapevine, TX, and Paper for Water. Thank you to the donors and volunteers who support these nonprofits. I am grateful for their dedication to changing the world, their inspirational leadership, and the work they do each day. Finally, I'd like to offer a special note of appreciation to Tula Weis for believing in this book to share the story of the next generation.

Contents

About the Author

Holly Hull Miori PhD, MPA, MTS, CFRE has spent nearly twenty years fundraising and is an elder millennial herself. She has raised funds both locally and nationally in areas as diverse as higher education, health care, social services, the arts, human rights, and Holocaust education. She has served on multiple local and national boards including Association of Fundraising Professionals (AFP), AFP Global Government Relations Committee, AWARE Dallas at The Dallas Foundation, and Paper for Water. She also teaches fundraising for graduates and undergraduates and is a sought-after speaker nationally and locally on topics as diverse as family foundations, millennial workforce, conscious capitalism, faith-based fundraising, ethical fundraising, and trends in philanthropy. She holds master's degrees in theological studies and public affairs and a PhD in public affairs, where she focused on millennial philanthropy. She is a past recipient of the ARNOVA Fellowship, a fellow of the Lake Institute at Indiana University Lilly Family School of Philanthropy, and is the co-owner of CTD Initiative, LLC. She has held the CFRE (Certified Fund Raising Executive) since 2012. She holds a master's and PhD in public affairs from The University of Texas at Dallas, a master's in theological studies from Brite Divinity School at Texas Christian University, and an undergraduate degree from Austin College in Sherman, TX.

List of Figures

List of Tables

1

Philanthropy and the Millennial Generation

This book is designed for the academic, the nonprofit executive, the fundraiser, and the inquisitive nonprofit volunteer. Inspired by my master's and dissertation at The University of Texas at Dallas, the goal of *Millennial Philanthropy: Next Generation Fund Development for Professionals and Nonprofits* is to offer the reader a practical guide to millennial philanthropy backed by research. As a professional fundraiser for over two decades, the goal of my academic research is to discover practical hands-on ways to engage 75 million potential philanthropists. As an (elder) millennial, I've come to appreciate the quirks, personalities, and inspiration of my entire generation. Through both quantitative and qualitative case studies, we will explore the role of millennials in the nonprofit and philanthropic landscape and provide practical advice for the fundraising and nonprofit community. And to answer the question of "what's next," we will end by taking a peek at Generation Z.

Defining Millennials

When diving into millennial research, there is some debate on which years define this generation, but many authors agree on the two decades spanning 1980–1999 (Twenge, Campbell, and Carter 2014). Although sometimes referred to as Generation Y (as they were located between Generations X and Z), the moniker "millennials" seemed to stick since the first cohort of the generation was coming of age (i.e., turned 20) at the millennium while

H. Hull Miori, *Millennial Philanthropy*,
https://doi.org/10.1007/978-3-031-30269-5_1

the last was being born (Weiler 2005). Some individuals (nicknamed "cuspers") who identify as millennials are on the "cusp" of each side of the cutoff years. Older members of the generation like myself are called "elders" or "elder millennials," and of course there are those who do not feel comfortable with the millennial label (Weiler 2005; DelCampo et al. 2017; Segers, Inceeoglue, and Finkelstein 2014).

Generations are important to discuss because they are a useful shorthand for individuals falling within a certain band of years and because generations share common historical touchpoints as they grew up while also having unique relationships with one another. Commonly acknowledged living generations include the Silent Generation (1928–1945), Baby Boomers (1946–1964), Generation X (1965–1979), Millennials (1980–1999), Generation Z (2000–2011), and now Alpha (2012–present) (Dimock 2019; Carter 2016; Sargeant and Shang 2017).

The Silent Generation (1928–1945) includes 35 million people. They grew up through the Great Depression and value stability. This generation also saw the emergence of white-collar jobs and the beginnings of widespread higher education (Sprague 2008, 1). The Silent Generation has high trust in institutions and grew up trusting the government (Rooney, Wang, and Ottoni-Wilhelm 2018, 921). This type of trust translated into trusting large nonprofits.

Baby Boomers (1946–1964) refer to the boom of births after World War II. This generation grew up experiencing monumental events like the man on the moon, significant figures like Martin Luther King, Jr. and the emergence of rock and roll groups like the Beatles (McIntosh-Elkins, McRitchie, and Scoones 2007). Baby Boomers have been referred to as highly motivated individuals (Fishman 2016, 255–56). The traditional family unit that Baby Boomers often experienced growing up included a working husband who connects the family to religion. The role of religion and marriage is especially tied together for this generation (Roof 2001, 218). This influenced how philanthropy was traditionally given; volunteerism was impacted as well since the family unit gave and volunteered as a unit.

Generation X (1965–1979) includes 57 million people and had a history of being "latchkey" kids, exposed to high rates of daycare and divorce (Rochester 2018, 1). The MTV generation are as a group both media-savvy and cynical. This group distrusts their elders, especially Baby Boomers (Sargeant 2005, 157). Sometimes called the Lost Generation, they desire a work-life balance and self-career development (Kian, Fauziah, and Yusoff 2012, 397–98). This generation is also most likely to own a business (Generation X Americans Born 1965 to 1976 2016, 6). These activities influence how they react to nonprofits and what they expect from these organizations—to be technologically savvy and utilize television and print as part of their communication. In addition, their distrust of leadership has crossed into the nonprofit community.

Millennials: Two Sides of the Same Coin

And then comes the Millennials (1980–1999)—the focus of this book. Defining moments for this generation include high school shootings like Columbine and September 11th (McIntosh-Elkins, McRitchie, and Scoones 2007, 241). These events also shape millennial outlooks, giving them an international scope and urgency focused on the greater good, with a concern for social justice and often mistrust for national organizations. This generation feels entitled to recognition and honor, often reflected in their desire to want a profession with a purpose (Fishman 2016, 251). Millennials want marketing that caters to them and connects with their values more than other generations (Mangiaforte n.d.). Yet marketing content developed to interest millennials must recognize the wide age range and how younger and elder millennials need different marketing styles (including social media platforms) (Mangiaforte n.d.).

The "Jekyll and Hyde" issues that emerge when looking closely at millennials create the groundwork for our study and impact their philanthropy, volunteerism, and outlook on life. This generation has come with several stereotypes that include having no money, being unconcerned with volunteering their time, being entitled, only concerned about the next like on social media, always worried about praise and the next trophy, and being extremely entrepreneurial. However, the studies will show a complex generation that comes at the issue of philanthropy and volunteerism from multiple perspectives and angles (Fig. 1.1).

Fig. 1.1 Photo Credit: Isabelle Miori

Side One	Side Two
• Future of philanthropy and society • Providing hope with their entrepreneurial style • Most diverse generation (impacting outlook) • Creative • Realistic • Pragmatic • Best educated generation • Focused on the greater good	• Overly self-focused • Narcissistic • Too involved with technology (can they look up from their devices??) • Care only about the next like on Facebook and other social media • Taking longer to marry (on average age 27 for women and 29 for men) • Feel lost • Seemingly lacking the "bigger picture"

Millennials and Philanthropy: More than Avocado Toast and Lattes

When I give talks on millennials and philanthropy, the top questions include (Fig. 1.2):

- Do they have money?
- Do they volunteer?
- How do we get their attention besides a happy hour or a fun background for social media?
- What do I do with my millennial intern?

Fig. 1.2 Photo Credit: Isabelle Miori

While I can't fix your intern problems, this book will navigate the first three questions and help you look at the millennial generation from a philanthropic, volunteer, and communications standpoint. The goal is to create a practical fundraising roadmap for the academic and fundraising community.

As the largest generation with 75.4 million people, millennials have an opportunity to make a significant impact on nonprofits and philanthropy (Ehley 2016). These individuals have their motivations, unique perceptions of philanthropy, and desires for genuine social change (Millennial Impact Report 2016). Scholars have shown that peer-to-peer influence is the largest lever in millennial decision-making with respect to philanthropy, though family and work colleagues still influence volunteerism and philanthropy (Landers 2018). The generation has been disappointed by previous generations and current events and is passionate to serve as advocates for their local communities (Millennial Impact Report 2016). In addition, as a racially diverse and well-educated generation, these individuals have an opportunity to make their mark on philanthropy. In the wake of 9/11, Hurricane Katrina, Black Lives Matter, COVID-19, and the age of technology, this generation is no longer aligning their philanthropic goals and approaches with those of their parents. Researchers have argued that millennials do not care about "tradition, status, tax advantage, or anything other than actual causes" (Jones 2021). They are not swayed by society papers, celebrity speakers, and expensive dinners. How then will nonprofits appeal to the hearts and wallets of this generation? As a fundraiser also, I find myself asking how will I best engage my peers now and in the years to come?

Initial research shows a complex generation that has been influenced by political unrest, environmental disasters, terrorism, and the 2007–2008 Great Recession. The fallout this generation continues to endure includes having to address the aftermath and unique challenges that come with so many shockwaves. The residual effects include distrust in the government, student loan debt, and housing dilemmas (millennialimpactreport.com). Recent events have shaken the assumption that even the most mundane parts of life can be taken for granted. Despite this upheaval, millennials have played formative roles amid the distress. For example, millennials played a critical part in the Black Lives Matter movement by taking a large role in the protests and showcasing the racial diversity that reflects their generation (Rendón 2020). And due to technological advancements, changes in this generation's attitudes regarding religion, politics, education, diversity, and philanthropy overlap and intertwine (Millennial Impact Report: 10 Years Looking Back 2020).

As the largest living generation, millennials are a fascinating group that deserves a deeper look when it comes to philanthropy. The nonprofit community has traditionally shied away from this generation, perhaps believing that they only concern themselves with avocado toast, lattes, and the next like on social media. But a closer look at millennials reveals that they donate, volunteer, and support nonprofits in a variety of capacities. The stereotypes need to be reframed. As Baby Boomers continue to age, they will pass on their accumulated wealth in their final days. The "silver tsunami" is occurring with the Great Transfer of Wealth—between 29.4 trillion and 65 trillion dollars to millennials by 2030 (Kelly 2019; Levitz 2021). This large transfer of wealth will impact millennials in the way they live, their debt, and, most importantly for us in the nonprofit community, their ability to donate.

Consider, for example, the fact that millennials are digital natives and expect nonprofits to have a digital presence, fast response time, be socially active, and have a global viewpoint even if they are only a local group. Nonprofits must reconfigure their fundraising and volunteer plans in light of these facts. Keela, a customer relationship management (CRM) company, suggests a fundraising plan with mobile-friendly communication tools, simplified donation tools, impactful donor stories, leveraged social media, engaged peer-to-peer contacts, and nurtured donor relationships (Jones 2021). The nonprofit can "use social media as a megaphone for their causes" which creates an opportunity to amplify the organization to the community (Perlstein n.d.). If a nonprofit can leverage the social media of a millennial, it can expand its reach even more than paid advertisements. As nonprofits look to the future, they should think ahead about how they will engage the millennial generation. In short, when asking why an organization needs to study millennial philanthropy, there is a lot to unpack!

This book will provide an analysis of millennials—a generation with growing influence—and evaluate their interaction with nonprofits in regard to fundraising and volunteerism. With three chapters devoted to two millennial case studies and another about Gen Z, the goal is to share new findings and review preconceived notions. The final chapter will also share practical steps for engaging millennials that moves beyond happy hours and online content.

Interview: Gabby Leon Spatt

Biography

Gabby Leon Spatt is the Director of Philanthropy at the Atlanta-based Hirsch Legacy Fund. With a career that has spanned for-profit and nonprofit roles, including a tech startup, SPANX by Sara Blakely and the Schusterman Family Foundation, Gabby knows community engagement is at the core of human flourishing and commits her time to organizations that share her values. Born and raised in Coral Springs, Florida, with a degree in Business and Nonprofit Organizational Leadership from the University of Florida, Gabby, her husband, and their young son call Atlanta, Georgia home.

What Is Your First Memory of Philanthropy?

I grew up with grandparents who always talked about supporting the community that has given you so much. They believed deeply in the idea of *tikkun olam*, the Jewish value for repairing the world, and influenced me to always make sure to give of my time, talent, and treasure.

What Is Your Family's Influence on Philanthropy?

My husband and I have been very intentional with our giving form, planning out where we want to give and why. It's made giving much more meaningful, fun, and easier to determine where our support goes each year. I also find myself fundraising for organizations I'm on the board of. It's a great feeling to share my work with friends and family.

What Is the Last Gift You Made and Why?

The last gift I made was to the Atlanta Chapter of the National Council of Jewish Women (NCJW) in honor of a mentor's 80th Birthday. She is a do-gooder (in the best possible way), mentor, and friend, and I was honored to plan an NCJW volunteer-oriented event for her birthday party at Second Helpings of Atlanta, where the group packed 2,000 meals for those in need.

What Has Been Your Favorite Gift?

My time supporting the American Jewish Committee (AJC) is by far my favorite gift I've given. From my first event with AJC at 25 years old, I knew AJC would be a place I would call home for many years. AJC has given me once-in-a-lifetime opportunities to travel and meet individuals worldwide, including my husband. AJC has taught me many skills around leadership, being on a board, advocacy, fundraising, and so much more.

How Did You Get Involved with the Nonprofits You Are Involved in?

Getting involved for me was easy. My network of friends, work, my synagogue, and some of the nonprofits I joined in college are membership organizations that provide volunteer opportunities for alumni to stay engaged.

How Many Nonprofits Are You Engaged in?

I have a knack for getting involved and having a hard time giving something up because it means so much to me. I'm currently involved with four nonprofits now in addition to my professional role, which is centered around philanthropy. I have held local, national, and global roles with the AJC, the leading global Jewish advocacy organization. At the National Council for Jewish Women's Atlanta Chapter, I am a board member overseeing the governance and programming of the organization. At my synagogue, I am a member of the Parents Teacher Association, and at Phi Mu Fraternity, I am a committee member of the volunteer experience committee, ensuring our hundreds of volunteers have a purposeful and meaningful experience.

How Did You Get Involved?

Each nonprofit organization has its reason for my involvement. The common reason among all is that they represent an interest or experience that connects with me and has kept me engaged and involved in various ways with my time, talent, and treasure.

Do You Raise Funds for These Nonprofits, Give Personally, or Both?

I do both! I understand that having a leadership role in a nonprofit organization comes with certain responsibilities, and giving a gift is one of them. My husband and I work together to decide where our donations go and what our philanthropy means to us. I've also spent many hours raising funds for organizations I'm a part of, which can be incredibly meaningful and a way to share my passions with friends and family.

What Is Your Generation's Biggest Influence in Philanthropy?

I think the millennial generation saw a transition of giving to many organizations instead of just a few. Maybe it's because we're indecisive or don't know how to say no, but we've been known for giving fewer dollars to a larger number of organizations.

What Do You Hope for Your Generation?

For my generation, the millennial generation, I hope we continue to expand on what philanthropy means and instill it as a necessary idea for generations to come. I also hope we recognize our ability to influence organizations for the better and continue to work hard to do so.

Spending Power: Why Care About Millennials

Millennials do almost everything online. They may go into a store, but will check prices online. You ask them for a philanthropic gift in the mail, but will make the gift online (or actually use your QR code!). They find their romantic partners online and find jobs online. But in the wake of COVID-19 and social movements that occurred, they are also looking for something more in their jobs, relationships, and even more with their interactions with their nonprofits. But how do fundraisers get their attention besides just going online?

Research on millennial philanthropy has been focused and not looked at the broad picture. The research has been focused on arts organizations and studying millennials through case studies in areas like art museums, social media, and corporate social responsibility initiatives (Robertson 2017; Grieshammer 2019; Kim and Austin 2019; Kavanaugh 2017). Other case studies have included those who have hit the jackpot and inherited wealth in the millennial generation (Goldseker and Moody 2020). These lessons are important, but lacking is an overview provided by industry and academia that studies the broad picture of millennial philanthropy. Existing studies provide details from the qualitative approach but do not provide a quantitative or mixed methods approach to offer a more rigorous examination. This book provides a notable exception: providing mixed methods look at examining the phenomenon of millennial philanthropy. Both qualitative and quantitative data are important for understanding 75 million potential philanthropists.

Even though the research is thin, we still need to understand what research there is on millennials and how they impact philanthropy. There is a belief from the general public that the generation may be immature; some even label the millennials as "Generation Me" (Twenge, Campbell, and Carter 2014). However, Twenge, Campbell, and Carter (2014) caution against blanket criticisms of millennials, as their attitudes could simply be based on their younger age. Some research describes them as "coming of age" as a generation. Of course each generation is complex with multiple sides or counterpoints (Twenge, Campbell, and Carter 2014), and every generation goes through a time of being young and "coming of age" where the young are "shaking out" their youth. The metaphor I will use in this book is a Rubik's cube, which is both complex and always changing. Since this generation is racially diverse in a global economy, each person in it is unique.

Millennials today have the reputation of being lazy and immature. But guess what? Your parents and your grandparents also had this reputation at one point. Previously, Baby Boomers and Generation X also received this moniker from their elders as each generation was dealing with life experiences and needing to mature (Twenge, Campbell, and Carter 2014, 70). In other words, while millennials are perceived as selfish, they may just be going through a "growing up" stage like every generation has done before them and will grow out of this stage as they get older. Nor are all millennials alike: Elder millennials turned 40 in 2020 and 2021 during a worldwide crisis, while at the same time younger members of this generation turned 20 and are just now leaving their teen years behind. The younger ones are finding internships, leaving college, and becoming members of the workforce. As researchers, employers, and fundraisers, we should note the size of the age range in the generation and be mindful of how a generation matures at its own pace.

With a generation having a range of twenty years, the millennial generation remembers pagers, floppy disks, and the dramatic changes in social media from MySpace, Facebook, Snapchat, TikTok, Instagram, and others. Millennials grew up with the first wave of computers in their homes but can also remember dial-up internet access. They emerged at the same time as the popularization of personal cell phones and the invention of the smartphone (King 2016, 2).

Research also shows that social media plays a critical role when discussing millennial engagement patterns with nonprofits. Nonprofits will not be successful without engaging the millennial generation through Facebook, Instagram, and other social media outlets (Saratovsky and Feldmann 2013). The patterns with technology rely on "referrals and guidance" from social networks that include "friends, family, and co-workers" (Saratovsky and Feldman 2013, 94). Determining engagement through social media involves comparing "self-benefits versus others-benefit" (Einolf 2016). In other words, the work is helping one's self versus helping others. However, though managing digital impressions are essential when thinking of public image, "We over Me" is also evident within this generation (Paulin et al. 2014, 343). This generation both uses social media but also values offline activities with a nonprofit (Paulin et al. 2014, 343–44).

One way to examine philanthropy is to look at average giving. This metric reviews the giving on average by year. As seen in Table 1.1, though different statistics were found, the similar ranges create a familiar narrative on how much millennials give annually:

Studies show that while millennials do not donate as much as Baby Boomers, what they give is still noteworthy. A gift of around five hundred dollars per millennial can still be significant for any nonprofit, especially if they recruit numerous millennials to the organization who donate annually. Research also shows that while millennials gave significantly less to religious nonprofits, their volunteerism is almost on par with Baby Boomers. Per

Table 1.1 Analysis of giving by generation

	Dunham + Co 2017 Avg. giving per year	Millennial Impact Report, (2015) Avg. giving per year
Millennials	$580	$481
Gen Xers	$799	$1,212
Boomers	$1,365	$732
Matures/Silent Generation	$1,093	–

Dunham + Company. 2017. "Millennial Donors: They're Not Who You Think They Are," 5; Millennial Impact Report (2015)

the Independent Sector, the value of a volunteer hour stands at $28.54 per hour in 2021 (Independent Sector Releases New Value of Volunteer Time of $28.54 Per Hour 2021) and millennials donate on average 40 hours per year (Millennial Impact Report 2016).

What Indicators Influence Philanthropy?

Previous research across social science disciplines has found that philanthropy is influenced by many characteristics: gender, marital and child status, religion, race, nationality, education, and age (Sargeant 2005, 62). A generation can be a useful construct through which to study giving because many of these traits are often influenced by age cohort. Shared experiences lead to political, economic, and social influences that can last a lifetime and impact people of the same generation in similar ways. In layman's terms, generations experience the same things together and feel a camaraderie. Millennials in particular are even more motivated by their shared experiences due to the overwhelming influence of social media and technology that kicked off during their formative years (Trobe 2013). Let's take a deeper dive into factors that particularly impact philanthropy for the millennial generation.

Gender

The different giving patterns between men and women within the millennial generation have been documented (Paulin et al. 2014, 344). Women are more likely to respond to helping others, while men are more concerned with "help-self" (Paulin et al. 2014, 339). Sargeant and Shang discuss how women, especially millennial women, prefer language that improves the world and helps society (Sargeant and Shang 2017, 542). When examining moral identity as another avenue for how to look at the generation, women gave their most significant gifts to an "outgroup" or in other words outside the nonprofit, while men, on the other hand, increasingly give to in-groups or by persons in the nonprofit. The current literature suggests that social media is critical for the success of nonprofits, which is used differently based on gender.

Work

Whether working for a nonprofit (which accounts for 10% of the overall workforce) or engaging with a nonprofit through their job (through volunteerism or a workplace giving campaign), work is a critical place to examine millennial philanthropy (Irs.org n.d.). Millennials are part of government, nonprofit, for-profit, organizations ("big corporation"), and public-public partnerships. At work millennials can gain access to opportunities to give through employee giving campaigns. While not workaholics, they envision their lives as the intersection of work and play—the communities they interact with both at work and home.

Religion

It's well known that religious donors donate more frequently than non-religious donors, give larger amounts, volunteer more, and understandably give to more religious causes (King, 2018). The majority of funds (as high as 73%) raised in the United States have religious ties ("Connected to Give: Smart Labs Report," 2013). This amount is significant and is roughly split between giving to congregations and organizations with religious ties (examples of religious ties include nonprofits founded by churches or those with faith-missions).

When you have a whole generation that is less religious than previous generations, it is important to consider the effect of the "millennial nones" on fundraising (Reed 2016, 155). Congregational attendance is a key measure of philanthropic motivation (King 2018), and the "nones" in this generation no longer attend a place of worship (Reed 2016, 155). Fundraising is, therefore, significantly impacted by the fact that congregational attendance is on the wane for millennials. The main philanthropic channel is cut off for this generation, likely leading to them giving less money and time than past generations who attended worship more regularly. But a changing market also offers an opportunity for fundraisers: Millennials need to be offered more appropriate indicators to trigger philanthropic motivation.

Social Justice

Millennials are an active social justice and social equity generation. This generation is both more racially diverse and racially tolerant than previous generations (Anderson and Rainie 2010, 9–10). Researchers even describe the post-racial season as being spearheaded by the millennial generation (Goldberg 2015). The Pew Research Center also reports that in 2014 67% of all millennials were also in favor of legalized same-sex marriage (Anderson and Rainie, 2010). Millennials "see" social issues rather than institutions (Millennial Impact Report: Ten Years Looking Back 2020). In short, millennials do not view the philanthropic world through the same social lens as previous generations and are more "activist" in their outlook. This generation also wants to see themselves in what they participate in for fundraising. The "representative bureaucracy" task of nonprofit organizations is to have their audience or their community see themselves (Riccucci and Saidel 1997; Brown and Kellough 2020). To attract the millennial base, nonprofits have to ask themselves how do their marketing materials represent the millennial generation in print and online?

Relationships

Millennials are involved with and influenced by social networking platforms more so than previous generations (Read et al. 2012; Anderson and Rainie 2010). These include (but are not limited to) Instagram, TikTok, Pinterest, Twitter, Snapchat, LinkedIn, and Reddit (and the list continues to evolve). More research is needed about millennial engagement with social media outlets like these and how this generation utilizes these outlets to engage with nonprofits (gender differences may exist for these different social media outlets, but not much public research exists on marketing differences). Despite being virtual, these networks also impact face-to-face and daily interaction and the role of philanthropy. For this generation, many philanthropic gifts happen through peer-to-peer fundraising or online.

Previous generations were highly influenced by their parents and this served as an influencer for giving. This impacted fundraising when discussing the intergenerational transfer of influence and funding. Parental influence—how the parents persuade and motivate their children—does not differ between millennials and Generation X (Einolf 2016, 437). Researchers have shown that millennials perceive their parents as more hands on and appreciative of the diversity in their community (Barroso, Parker, and Bennett 2020). In regard to developmental parental influence, the question remains regarding how much influence parents provide for philanthropic behavior (including funding preferences, amounts, and donor priorities).

Economic and Political Change

Numerous sources agree that millennials are better educated, more empathetic, embrace social media, yet are slower to settle down compared to other generations (King 2016, 1–3; Anderson and Rainie 2010, 9). Additionally, the Great Recession from 2007 to 2008 hit the older millennials hard since many were unable to find full employment. They graduated from college with minimal job prospects, so they jumped into graduate school in record numbers. This created additional student loan debt while not necessarily increasing job prospects (Anderson and Rainie 2010, 7). This student loan debt could impact their overall capacity to give.

Compared to Generation X, millennials are more active politically (including volunteerism) (Einolf 2016, 436). One interesting finding shows that for millennials volunteerism can be a substitute for voting; at the same time, the desire for transparency in government reveals an underlying interest to be active in the community ("When It Comes to Politics, Do Millennials Care About Anything?" n.d.). The role of volunteerism continues to tie into philanthropy as it can be an indicator for giving but also (as we will explore further) a substitute for giving.

Overview of the Book

Before we dive into the work of the millennial and Generation Z case studies, the second chapter looks at the nonprofit landscape. It includes the history of the generations we will study, examines the different types of nonprofits and where their money comes from, and looks at the metrics for how fundraising is measured. As we ask "What's Next?" in our work in the nonprofit community, understanding the framework of the philanthropic landscape will illuminate the particulars regarding the qualitative and quantitative millennial and Generation Z case studies.

The third chapter looks at a millennial philanthropic organization—BvB Dallas (formerly Blondes vs. Brunettes)—through qualitative interviews. This chapter provides a sneak peek into the millennial mindset by looking at the individuals within the group regarding how they think about philanthropy and volunteering. By taking a deep dive into these millennials' giving and volunteering behaviors and patterns, the nonprofit and academic community can begin to understand the millennial mentality.

The fourth chapter examines volunteerism by looking at a social services agency—GRACE (formerly Grapevine Relief and Community Exchange)—through a quantitative approach. It takes a deep dive into millennial behavior by asking questions about volunteerism and different activities that can impact giving and philanthropy. The fifth chapter returns to GRACE to study philanthropic differences between generations. This quantitative chapter will show the role of different giving patterns in relation to events like galas and return to the role volunteerism has on philanthropy.

The sixth chapter looks ahead at Generation Z through a case study of Paper for Water, a group that uses origami to engage a younger generation and "bring water to the thirsty." This Generation Z-based organization reveals insights about the next generation of philanthropists and volunteers regarding how this generation gives, volunteers, and engages nonprofits differently.

The final concluding chapter will provide practical advice for the nonprofit community, fundraisers, boards, and volunteers on how to prepare for the next generation. It looks at ramifications for communications, volunteerism, brand awareness, events, social networking, and philanthropy, and how they all interconnect. The chapters will also have interviews with the next generation throughout the book to help us deep dive into their thinking about philanthropy and volunteerism.

As a fundraiser and academic, my goal is to provide both an academic textbook but also a practical guide for the nonprofit community and fundraisers, boards, and volunteers on how to prepare for the next generation who candidly have already arrived.

References

Anderson, Janna, and Lee Rainie. 2010. "Millennials Will Make Online Sharing in Networks a Lifelong Habit." Pew Research. Accessed December 14, 2022. https://www.pewresearch.org/internet/2010/07/09/millennials-will-make-online-sharing-in-networks-a-lifelong-habit/.

Barroso, Amanda, Kim Parker, and Jesse Bennett. May 27, 2020. "As Millennials Near 40, They're Approaching Family Life Differently Than Previous Generations." Accessed August 28, 2021. https://www.pewresearch.org/social-trends/2020/05/27/as-millennials-near-40-theyre-approaching-family-life-differently-than-previous-generations/.

Brown, Lawrence A., and J. Edward Kellough. 2020. "Contracting and the Bureaucratic Representation of Minorities and Women: Examining Evidence from Federal Agencies." *Review of Public Personnel Administration* 40, no. 3: 447–67.

Carter, Christine Michel. December 21, 2016. "The Complete Guide to Generation Alpha, the Children of Millennials." Accessed August 28, 2021. https://www.forbes.com/sites/christinecarter/2016/12/21/the-complete-guide-to-generation-alpha-the-children-of-millennials/?sh=226ed2036236.

Charities and Nonprofits A-Z Site Index. n.d. Accessed March 17, 2021. Ncss.urban.org.

Connected to Give: Smart Labs Report. 2013. Accessed March 17, 2021. https://jumpstartlabs.org/offering/research-reports/connected-to-give/#:~:text=The%20Connected%20to%20Give%20report,religious%20and%20non%2Dreligious%20Americans.

DelCampo, Robert G., Lauren A. Haggerty, and Lauren Ashley Knippel. 2017. *Managing the Multi-Generational Workforce: From the GI Generation to the Millennials*. Routledge.

Dimock, Michael. January 17, 2019. Defining Generations: Where Millennials End and Generation Z Begins. Accessed December 14, 2022. https://www.pewresearch.org/fact-tank/2019/01/17/where-millennials-end-and-generation-z-begins/.

Dunham + Company. 2017. "Millennial Donors: They're Not Who You Think They Are." Accessed May 30, 2017. https://www.dunhamandcompany.com/.

Ehley, Brianna. 2016. "Millennials Dethrone Baby Boomers as Largest Generation." Accessed December 14, 2022. https://www.politico.com/story/2016/04/millennials-largest-generation-222448.

Einolf, Christopher. 2016. "Millennials and Public Service Motivation: Finding from a Survey of Master's Degree Students." *Public Administration Quarterly* 40, no. 3: 429–57.

Fishman, Ann Arnof. 2016. "How Generational Differences Will Impact America's Aging Workforce: Strategies for Dealing with Aging Millennials, Generation X, and Baby Boomers." *Strategic HR Review* 15, no. 6: 250–57.

Generation X Americans Born 1965 to 1976. 6th ed. New Strategist Publications, 2009.

Goldberg, David Theo. 2015. *Are we all postracial yet*? John Wiley & Sons.

Goldseker, Sharna, and Michael Moody. 2020. *Generation Impact: How Next Gen Donors Are Revolutionizing Giving*. John Wiley & Sons.

Grieshammer, Natalie. 2019. "Engaging Millennial Philanthropy in Art Museums Through an Online Platform." PhD diss., University of Akron.

"Independent Sector Releases New Value of Volunteer Time of $28.54 Per Hour." April 20, 2021. Accessed September 14, 2021. https://independentsector.org/news-post/independent-sector-releases-new-value-of-volunteer-time-of-28-54-per-hour/

Jones, Ryan. February 26, 2021. "Millennial Giving: How to Reach Gen Z and Millennial Donors." Accessed September 11, 2021. https://www.keela.co/blog/nonprofit-resources/millennial-giving.

Kavanaugh, Karen. 2017. "Gamification Techniques and Millennial Generation Philanthropy." PhD diss., Walden University.

Kelly, Jack. 2019. "Millennials Will Become Richest Generation In American History As Baby Boomers Transfer Over Their Wealth." Accessed September 11, 2021. https://www.forbes.com/sites/jackkelly/2019/10/26/millennials-will-become-richest-generation-in-american-history-as-baby-boomers-transfer-over-their-wealth/?sh=3cb879f76c4b.

Kian, Tan Shen, and Wan Fauziah Wan Yusoff. 2012. "Generation X and Y and Their Work Motivation." In *Proceedings International Conference of Technology Management, Business and Entrepreneurship*, pp. 396–408.

Kim, Seoyeon, and Lucinda Austin. 2019. "Effects of CSR Initiatives on Company Perceptions Among Millennial and Gen Z Consumers." *Corporate Communications: An International Journal* 25, no. 2: 299–317.

King, David P. 2016. "Millennials, Faith and Philanthropy: Who Will Be Transformed?" *Bridge/Work* 1, no. 1: 1–10.

King, David P. 2018. "Values and Giving." Dallas-Fort Worth Association of Fundraising Conference, Irving, TX, June 15, 2018.

Landers, Linda. 2018. "Top Strategies for Marketing to Millennial Women." Accessed September 4, 2021. https://girlpowermarketing.com/strategies-for-marketing-to-millennial-women/.

Levitz, Eric. Will The Great Wealth Transfer' Trigger a Millennial Civil War? 2021. *New York Magazine*. Accessed September 1, 2021. https://nymag.com/intelligencer/2021/07/will-the-great-wealth-transfer-spark-a-millennial-civil-war.html.

Mangiaforte, Lauren. n.d. "8 Tips on How to Market Effectively to Millennial Women." Accessed September 4, 2021. https://insights.newscred.com/8-tips-on-how-to-market-effectively-to-millennial-women/.

McIntosh-Elkins, Jeni, Karen McRitchie, and Maureen Scoones. 2007. "From the Silent Generation to Generation X, Y and Z: Strategies for Managing the generation mix." In *Proceedings of the 35th Annual ACM SIGUCCS Fall Conference*, 240–46.

Millennial Impact Report 2015. 2015. Accessed May 30, 2017. http://www.themillennialimpact.com/past-research.

Millennial Impact Report 2016. 2016. Accessed May 30, 2017. http://www.themillennialimpact.com/past-research.

Millennial Impact Report: 10 Years Looking Back. 2020. Accessed May 30, 2017. http://www.themillennialimpact.com/latest-research.

Paulin, Michèle, Ronald J. Ferguson, Kaspar Schattke, and Nina Jost. 2014. "Millennials, Social Media, Prosocial Emotions, and Charitable Causes: The Paradox of Gender Differences." *Journal of Nonprofit & Public Sector Marketing* 26, no. 4: 335–53.

Perlstein, Greg. n.d. "Young People Want to Change the World. Nonprofits Can Help Them." Accessed September 11, 2021. https://www.theatlantic.com/sponsored/salesforceorg-2020/young-people-want-to-change-nonprofits-help/3454/.

Read, Pam, Chirag Shah, Lupita S-O'Brien, and Jaqueline Woolcott. 2012. "'Story of One's Life and a Tree of Friends'—Understanding Millennials' Information Behaviour in Social Networks." *Journal of Information Science* 38, no. 5: 489–97.

Reed, Randall. 2016. "A Book for None? Teaching Biblical Studies to Millennial Nones." *Teaching Theology & Religion* 19, no. 2: 154–74.

Rendón, María G. July 20, 2020. "Broad Support for Black Lives Matter Shows a New Generation of Race Consciousness Has Arrived." Accessed August 28, 2021. https://calmatters.org/commentary/my-turn/2020/07/broad-support-for-black-lives-matter-shows-a-new-generation-of-race-consciousness-has-arrived/.

Riccucci, Norma M., and Judith R. Saidel. 1997. "The Representativeness of State-Level Bureaucratic Leaders: A Missing Piece of the Representative Bureaucracy Puzzle." *Public Administration Review* 57, no. 5: 423–30.

Robertson, Suzanne. 2017. "The Millennial Generation and Philanthropy: The Time for Engagement Is Now." Masters thesis, Goucher College.

Rochester, Colin. 2018. "Trends in Volunteering." Volunteer Now.

Roof, Wade Clark. *Spiritual Marketplace: Baby Boomers and the Remaking of American Religion.* Princeton University Press, 2001.

Rooney, Patrick M., Xiaoyun Wang, and Mark Ottoni-Wilhelm. 2018. "Generational Succession in American Giving: Donors Down, Dollars Per Donor Holding Steady but Signs That It Is Starting to Slip." *Nonprofit and Voluntary Sector Quarterly* 47, no. 5: 918–38.

Saratovsky, Kari Dunn, and Derrick Feldmann. 2013. *Cause for Change: The Why and How of Nonprofit Millennial Engagement*. 1st ed. Jossey-Bass.

Sargeant, Adrian. 2005. "Church and Parachurch Fundraising in the United States: What Can We Learn?" *Journal of Philanthropy and Marketing* 10, no. 3: 133–36.

Sargeant, Adrian, and Jen Shang. 2017. *Fundraising Principles and Practice*. Vol. 17. John Wiley & Sons.

Segers, Jesse, Ilke Inceeoglue, and Lisa Finkelstein. 2014. "The Age Cube of Work." *Generational Diversity at Work: New Research Perspectives.* Ed. Emma Parry. Routledge.

Sprague, Caroline. 2008. "The Silent Generation meets Generation Y: How to Manage a Four-Generation Workforce with Panache." Talent Strategy, Human Capital Institute White Paper, 1–15.

Trobe, Rebecca. 2013. "A Qualitative Study of What Motivates Young Adults of the Millennial Generation Toward Philanthropy." PhD diss., The Wright Institute.

Twenge, Jean M., W. Keith Campbell, and Nathan T. Carter. 2014. "Declines in Trust in Others and Confidence in Institutions Among American Adults and Late Adolescents, 1972–2012." *Psychological Science* 25, no. 10: 1914–23.

Weiler, Angela. 2005. "Information-Seeking Behavior in Generation Y Students: Motivation, Critical Thinking, and Learning Theory." *The Journal of Academic Librarianship* 31, no. 1: 46–53.

"When It Comes to Politics, Do Millennials Care About Anything?" n.d. *The Atlantic*. Accessed July 11, 2021. https://www.theatlantic.com/sponsored/allstate/when-it-comes-to-politics-do-millennials-care-about-anything/255/.

2

The Nonprofit Landscape: How to Prepare for the Future

Philanthropy is a worldwide phenomenon that has a global impact, but for the purposes of this book we will focus on the United States. Philanthropy has a history that is centuries old, coming from individuals, corporations, and foundations. Philanthropy is also big business, supporting 10% of the workforce (TED Economics Daily 2018). Understanding how nonprofits view the philanthropic landscape is crucial to understanding millennial philanthropy.

History of Philanthropy

The history of philanthropy aligns with charity work in America. While recognizing there were other motivations for giving, for many religious obligations from the Abrahamic-based religions (Judaism, Christianity, and Islam) provided the context for giving (Bremner 1988, xii). Colonists began populating America against a historical backdrop of governments mingling church and state (Friedman and McGarvie 2003). Moving across a new land meant a sense of individualism prevailed (Hadenius 2015, 1), yet Protestant ideas and ethics influenced the support of the poor, orphans, and the homeless (Bremner 1988, xii; Friedman and McGarvie 2003). In the 1660s, Princeton offered "corn scholarships" where one-fifth of the students were supported by the proceeds from sales of corn to community members (Gaudiani 2004, 36). All of these influences also occurred during the era of colonization. Recognizing the important role of the first persons and Native

H. Hull Miori, *Millennial Philanthropy*,
https://doi.org/10.1007/978-3-031-30269-5_2

American community in the framework of our country also plays a role in the history of the United States.

As a British colony reacting to the feudal system, then to taxes levied in response to the French-American war, the United States has a unique past, creating a journey rooted in response to the government (Hadenius 2015, 4). These events resulted in the Declaration of Independence, creating political stability through a document of grievances (Hadenius 2015, 4). American exceptionalism's ideals are embedded in the lack of feudal systems and the rise of capitalism and less government (Lipset and Marks 2000, 24). These factors created an aversion to redistributive policies by the government, which impacted philanthropy and led to nonprofits taking a leading role in caring for the community.

Alongside the "strength of religion [and] weakness of a central state" in America at this time were "ethnic and racial diversity" and the diffusion of anti-feudal ideals (Lipset and Marks 2000, 16). In 1790 there were five major nationality groups and dozens of smaller ones (Raab and Lipset 1995, 10). At the same time, the economic success of the Puritans was derived from their embrace of capitalism with "rationality, hard work, savings and a strong achievement drive" (Raab and Lipset 1995, 13). Though a double-edged sword, the lack of a social class system created the groundwork for individualism (Lipset 1996, 67–75). The goal of philanthropies was to fund the communities' basic needs, placing the funding burden on the community.

The 1800s ushered in an age of benevolence that reflected American exceptionalism and Protestant ideals, which set the tone in the country toward government and philanthropy (Lipset 1996, 22–26). The highly influential *Democracy in America*, published in 1835 by Alexis de Tocqueville, observed that when an individual supports the community, the needs of all individuals will be served (Tocqueville and Reeve 1899). The goal he saw Americans pursuing was to have a better society with educated citizens who can support the greater good (Hadenius 2015, 2). This benevolence can be seen throughout the 1800s with workhouses for the poor and the spread of groups that served society (Bremner 1988, 58).

After the Civil War, the country underwent a shift with its first millionaires (Zunz 2014, 8). During this time, we see famous names like Andrew Carnegie, Cornelius Vanderbilt, John D. Rockefeller, and Henry Ford emerge, as well as the King and Kleberg families and Joseph Pew. These philanthropists in their time built legacies—many through unscrupulous means. However, they also created large-scale wealth holdings that still impact the economy generations later—including philanthropy.

While philanthropy is not a novel idea in the United States and even has roots before a formalized government, the idea of mass philanthropy and the collective good began to emerge in the 1920s (Zunz 2014; Friedman and McCarvie 2003). In 1929 we see the first family foundation (the Ford Foundation) which still exists today. The Great Depression and World War II resulted in an increased reliance on the state (Lipset 1996, 22). During this time groups like community chests and federations begin to form (American Religion Timelines 2022).

The philanthropic landscape changed with the era. World War II caused the professionalization of coordinated efforts in meeting wartime needs for "money, supplies and service" (A History of Modern Philanthropy: 1930–1980 2022). By the 1940s and 1950s, however, these legacy foundations had lost much of their interest in the improvement of K-12 education (Katz and Soskis 2018, 23). Legislation and legal cases like the Brown vs. Board of Education Supreme Court decision in 1954 also impacted the giving framework, shifting the focus of education funding and other policy decisions (How Philanthropy Diverts Social Movements 2019). The work continued with the 1964 Civil Rights Act and 1965 Voting Rights Act which influenced civil rights philanthropy and the role of the movement toward equity (How Philanthropy Diverts Social Movements 2019). Due to mistrust in the government, there emerged a growing shift to lean on nonprofits and hence philanthropy (Katz and Soskis 2018, 19). The philanthropy landscape changed further in the 1980s with individual giving serving as 80% of all giving—a 68% growth between 1955 and 1980. In the 1990s, the number of nonprofits dramatically skyrocketed from 422,000 in 1987 to 734,000 in 1998 (Candid 2001). During this period, the competition among nonprofits changed dramatically in the United States.

With the economic recession of 2001–2002 following 9/11, wealth became even more concentrated (Gaudiani 2004, 36). Although the subsequent 2007–2008 Great Recession led to a slow recovery as the housing market rose and fell during this time, in 2010 the extremely wealthy began signing the Giving Pledge. Started by Bill Gates, Melinda French Gates, and Warren Buffett, the goal was to have billionaires donate at least half of their estates. As of 2022, there are 236 signers (About the Giving Pledge 2022).

The philanthropy market had its first dip in the next decade in 2018 (when corrected for inflation). According to the *USA Giving Report*, philanthropy ebbed 1.7%, believed to be caused by tax reform with fewer persons itemizing as well as different donation patterns. However, groups and individuals gave $449.6 billion in philanthropy in 2020 (up from $410 billion in 2018) despite the pandemic (Giving USA 2018, 2020).

Overview of Nonprofit Community

Nonprofits serve our communities. Donors, board members, and volunteers work together to support the missions and values of these organizations that serve our community. They feed our hungry, educate our kids, shelter our neighbors, help the sick, and support our favorite arts projects. Approximately 1.54 million nonprofits (also known as the "third sector") were registered with the Internal Revenue Service in 2021—an increase of 4.5% since 2006 (Internal Revenue Service n.d.; Candid 2021; Sargeant and Shang 2017, 2). Nonprofits contributed $1.047 trillion to the US economy in 2016—an estimated 5.6% of the country's gross domestic product (Internal Revenue Service n.d.). In addition, the nonprofit sector is the third-largest in the workforce with 12.5 million workers (2020 Nonprofit Employment Report).

In 2020, philanthropic giving in the United States totaled $471.44 billion, including 69% from individuals, 19% from foundations, 9% from bequests, and 4% from corporations. *The Giving USA 2019* report shares that faith-based philanthropy makes up 29% of giving and includes "congregations, denominations, missionary societies, and religious media" (Giving USA 2019). Religious giving is the largest type of philanthropy per the *Giving USA 2019* report, though donations to other areas also serve the community throughout the years (Giving USA 2019).

These nonprofits support their annual budgets through revenue sources that may include government contracts, service fees, corporate donations, individual contributions, and foundation grants (Foster and Fine 2007). By looking at these areas of funding, a nonprofit can begin to plan ahead with respect to its philanthropy and fundraising plans. Many nonprofits are trying to engage with the next generation of philanthropists, which includes the millennial generation.

Throughout the years, the Great Depression, social movements, 9/11, the Great Recession, and the COVID-19 pandemic have created a need to study trends in philanthropy. There are concerns that millennials in particular do not donate for the same reasons or to the same causes as previous generations, but this has not been examined in the research literature—hence the need for this book!

Nonprofits come in all forms and sizes. Some are highly organized structures in multiple states with a large endowment, while others are small organizations that are barely hanging on. Based on the 2018 IRS data, nearly 50% are at $1 million in revenue based on nearly 210,000 submitted 990s (SOI Tax Stats 2022) (Fig. 2.1).

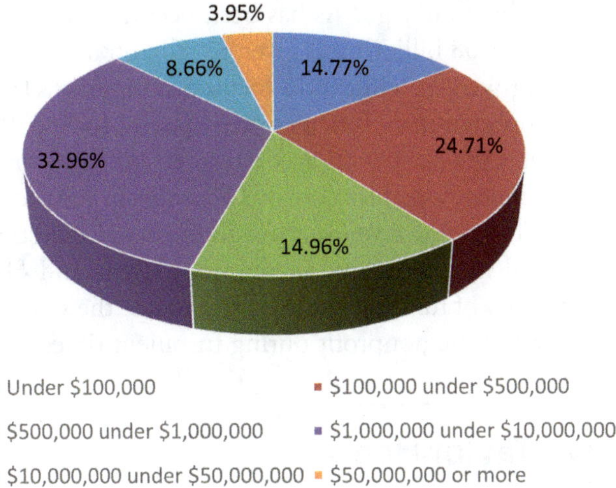

Fig. 2.1 Nonprofit sizes per IRS 2018 data

Fundraising serves as a large part of the revenue of most nonprofits, but the category of nonprofit indicates a group's tax status, not a budget strategy. Nonprofits generate revenue through membership fees, client services, products sold, and funds raised. How nonprofits raise revenue varies widely, from black-tie fundraising events to selling cookies. In 2019, donations to nonprofits totaled $427.71 billion in the United States (Giving USA 2019).

The United States IRS office has more than 30 classifications of tax-exempt organizations (Other Tax-Exempt Organizations 2022). Whether the nonprofit is local, regional, national, or international, the focus of most organizations falls into one of seven areas (Sargeant and Shang 2017; charitynavigator.org 2022):

- Animal Arts.
- Environmental.
- Health.
- International NGO (non-governmental organization).
- Culture.
- Education.
- Religion.

Nonprofits may also fall into more than one category. For example, a faith-based organization can provide social services, and an art museum may serve an educational purpose in the community.

But where does the money go? As has been occurring for decades, a large portion (28% or $131.08 billion) was given to religion in 2020. In that same year, 15% of giving went to education-focused nonprofits, 14% to human services, 12% to foundations, 10% to benefit public society, 9% to health, 5% to international affairs, 4% to arts, culture, and humanities, and 3% to environment/animals. Organizations fundraise from individuals, corporations, and foundations, earn revenue, have interest and investment payouts, have volunteers, and have in-kind contributions (Renz and Herman 2010, 485–90). The diversity of funding streams can provide the stability to support the long-term needs of the nonprofit during turbulent times

Interview: Taylor Hearn

Biography

Taylor Hearn is a 28-year-old Major League baseball pitcher from Royse City, TX. He has played for the Pittsburgh Pirates and is currently the pitcher for the Texas Rangers. His parents Robby and Debra, sister Robyn and fiancée' Andrea Hawkins all participate alongside him in his philanthropy. Taylor serves the community through events with the Texas Rangers Baseball Club, Texas Rangers Baseball Foundation, and The Player Alliance as well as hosting events such as a Christmas shopping spree for children in Royce City, Shopping with a Pro with Dick's Sporting Goods, feeding the homeless at The Arlington Life Shelter and hosting youth baseball camps and pitching workshops with athletes at the Texas Rangers Youth Academy (just to name a few!) in addition to supporting his hometown.

What Is Your First Memory of Philanthropy?

Being an active participant in the Fellowship of Christian Athletes (FCA) in high school and going through the minor leagues, I observed veterans giving back to the community and knew I wanted to make an impact and become the kind of person the younger generation would look up as well as help young athletes excel at their sport.

What Is Your Family's Influence on Philanthropy?

My family has always been there to lend a hand and help others in need through church, neighbors, the local community, and baseball.

How Did You Get Involved with the Nonprofits You Are Involved in?

My friends, family, work, place of worship, networking group—even my teammates have gotten me involved.

What Is Your Generation's Biggest Influence in Philanthropy?

Connecting with kids on video games and social media.

How Many Nonprofits Are You Engaged in?

I'm in the process of establishing my own foundation but involved in Texas Rangers Baseball Foundation, Texas Rangers MLB Urban Academy, The Players Alliance, Alzheimer's Association, AWARE AFFAIR and AWARE Dallas, local children's hospitals, schools, Arlington Life Shelter, and numerous youth baseball programs.

Do You Raise Funds for These Nonprofits, Give Personally, or Both?

Both.

What Do You Hope for Your Generation?

My hope for my generation is for each person to pay it forward and help others and the community to be a better place.

What Has Been Your Personal Favorite Gift?

Seeing the smile on children's faces and sharing my love of baseball with the next generation.

To What Organizations Do People Give?

Foundations

Foundations come in two different forms: public and private (Foundation Basics n.d.; Council of Foundations: Family Foundation n.d.). Public foundations include "funds from multiple unrelated donors" (Sargeant and Shang 2010, 463), whereas private foundations are funded by a small group of donors. The IRS defines the role of "public" charities since the public can donate to the organization (Charities and Nonprofits A-Z Site Index n.d.). Private foundations by contrast are not open to public donations and are focused on helping support the interests of a particular individual, family, or corporation (Foundation Basics n.d.; Sargeant and Shang 2010). Whereas corporate foundations support the initiatives of a corporation (Foundation Basics n.d.), individual foundations are often called family foundations and represent 90% of all foundations (Sargeant and Shang 2010, 463). According to the Council on Foundations, family foundation philanthropy is valued at $300 billion annually. Often, family foundations involve multiple generations in selecting nonprofits for fund distribution (Council of Foundations: Family Foundations n.d.).

Family foundations will be impacted by millennials in two ways: as the Baby Boomer generation ages out of leadership positions, more of them will be run by millennials, and as a result of the Great Transfer of Wealth from Boomers, more millennials will be the beneficiaries of wealth transfers (with the amount ranging from $29.4 trillion to $65 trillion dollars by 2030; see Kelly 2019; Levitz 2021). This affluence could greatly impact future giving through family foundations (Eisen and Tergesen 2021), as they make a dramatic impact on the national and international landscape, often making gifts over multiple years. They serve as a backdrop for funding across all sectors, including healthcare, education, arts, NGOs, social, legal, and environment at local, regional, national, and international levels. The function, roles of paid administrators, organizational structure, and even the mission values and goals could evolve when the next generation begins participating in the grantmaking process.

Donor-Advised Funds

Donor-Advised Funds (DAFs) are alternatives to private foundations (Tempel et al. 2016, 493). No longer does a family have to navigate the administrative burden of a family foundation. DAFs can be held at public charities, at local community foundations, and even "gift funds" at financial firms like Fidelity and Charles Schwab (Tempel et al. 2016, 494). Per the IRS, a DAF is a "separately identified fund or account that is maintained and operated by a section 501(c)(3) organization, which is called a sponsoring organization" (Philanthropy Roundtable 2021). Per Philanthropy Roundtable, the largest fundholders of DAFs from 2015 to 2019 include Fidelity Charitable, Vanguard Charitable, Schwab Charitable, and the National Philanthropic Trust (Philanthropy Roundtable 2021). These fund types are important as we look ahead to the Great Transfer of Wealth and where funds are held.

What Types of Giving Exist?

Fundraising efforts happen in a variety of ways and play a pivotal role for nonprofits. They can use a variety of means spanning recurring giving and social media to provide inspiration and build a case for support to expand fundraising.

A comprehensive fundraising plan for a nonprofit typically includes annual gifts, major/leadership gifts, capital campaign gifts, planned gifts, and in-kind fundraising. The Fundraising School has the best visual of this fundraising model, calling it the "Four-Legged Stool of Fundraising" (Tempel et al. 2016, 218) (Fig. 2.2).

Annual Giving

For nonprofits, annual giving encourages the same donors to make gifts year after year. Often an organization will obtain annual fund gifts by soliciting donors through a combination of direct mail and social media. Organizations work with annual giving in a coordinated fashion, often even naming

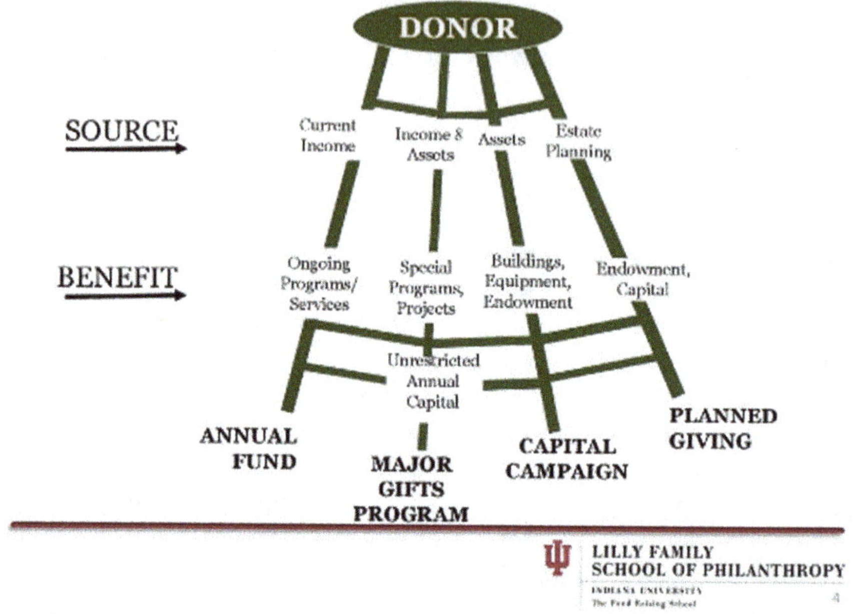

Fig. 2.2 4-Legged stool of fundraising

the fund with a recognizable term such as "Friends Fund." Larger organizations may name the program after important founders or donors of the organization like the Clara Barton Society for the American Red Cross and the Charles E. Diehl Society at Rhodes College (Clara Barton n.d; Annual Fund Giving Societies 2022). As organizations continue to professionalize, they may also consider launching monthly giving programs, also known as sustainer programs (Sargeant 2005, 35). Recurring gifts are when someone gives an automated gift on a regular basis, such as monthly or annually ("Recurring Gifts" 2021; "Recurring Membership Fees" 2021). Recurring gifts also help an organization prepare and plan for the future and annual fund donors also create a pathway for larger gifts for capital projects (Tempel et al. 2016, 75; Sargeant and Shang 2010, 35).

Major Gifts Program

Major gifts are the next level and type of giving. For most organizations, major gifts provide the "majority of an organization's income" (Sargeant 2005, 352). Major gifts are critical to an organization because 80% of major gifts are given by 20% of their donors. Each organization has a different threshold for a major gift. Some organizations split their major gifts into two segments to create a hierarchy of leadership gifts. These major gifts are often earmarked for programs (Tempel et al. 2016, 218).

Capital Campaign

A capital campaign "meets the organization's needs for increasing its assets" (often physical), has a fixed timeline and budget, and can also enhance endowments (Tempel et al. 2016; Sargeant and Shang 2017, 35). These campaigns tend to be large and can range from $50,000 to billions of dollars depending on the size of the organization. Capital campaigns leverage marketing funds to build out public relations and focus donors on organizational priorities.

Planned Giving

Bequests or planned gifts also are important. This type of fundraising includes bequests, beneficiary designations, charitable gift annuities, and charitable trusts (Tempel et al. 2016, 259). All of these vehicles offer opportunities for a donor to share their values in a long-term fashion. For some, the capital gains tax is avoided while also supporting their favorite charities.

In-Kind Donations

Finally (as part of the larger fundraising plan) are in-kind donations. Though not an individual leg as they cross categories, these include tangible assets a nonprofit agrees to accept (as major gifts, planned giving, or even as part of a capital campaign). Examples of tangible items include personal collections of arts, books, movies, cars, boats, aircraft, and equipment. Intangible items may include patents, copyrights for literary works, and copyright works under development, among others (Regents' Rules and Regulations 2004; utsystem.edu 2004). A strong gift policy will continue to support these types of donations.

How Nonprofits Measure Philanthropy

Even an established nonprofit must have metrics to measure the impact of fundraising activities. Nonprofits utilize a number of ways to estimate and measure donor loyalty to an organization including predictive modeling, which helps identify "constituents that are higher likelihood to engage, donate, lapse or renew" their giving (MacLaughlin 2016, 30). As the nonprofit continues to balance transactional and relationship approaches that support donor retention, lifetime value (LTV), donor relationships, long-term goals, and major emphasis is calculated (Sargeant and Shang 2017, 335).

Lifetime Transactions

The transactional side of the donor relationship comes from calculating the lifetime value to the organization (MacLaughlin 2016). An organization can see how much the person has invested in the organization over time. For example, Donor 1 may have invested $10,000 one-time while Donor 2 may have invested multiple times over 20 years with a giving total of $65,000. Donor 2 is of more value to the organization based on the donor's LTV. An organization may also analyze the frequency of individual donor gifts during a period, most frequently measured in a 12-month period. As yet another way of data modeling, a nonprofit can also measure a gift count, which shows the number of donor gifts. When shifting to a campaign focus, the nonprofit can look at return on investment (ROI), which equals immediate revenue generated against the cost of the acquisition campaign (Sargeant and Shang 2017, 342).

RFM

RFM stands for recency, frequency, and monetary, and is a common industry measure of attachment to an organization or nonprofit. Recency determines how recently a person donated to the organization. For example, the donor may have made a donation a few weeks ago or several years ago. Knowing the donors' most recent gift date shows their recent interest in the organization. The frequency is an important metric to show loyalty to the nonprofit. In other words, how embedded is the person or family into the nonprofit reveals a loyalty factor. Even for-profits utilize similar strategies by analyzing data from "frequent shopper" cards similar to those from grocery stores and cinemas. Monetary gifts are critical to understanding how much the donor donated. A donor who gives $5 versus $1 million plays a decidedly different factor in revenue (Birkholz 2020; Nandeshwar and Devine 2018; Heldt, Silveira, and Luce 2021). The depth of the relationship is a meaningful factor when the gift has different levels. Several tools calculate these scores automatically, but the scoring can also be calculated in Excel or software like R or STATA. RFM is also used in fundraising and fundraising software products like Raiser's Edge/Blackbaud, Bloomerang, Abila, and others.

Donor Research

Prospect donor research is used to help support the planning for a professional fundraising office. Wealth screens support fundraising initiatives by analyzing predictive factors to determine potential giving amounts. This information can provide wealth indicators and also highlight the interest of potential donors. With this information in hand, an organization can better focus "staff time and financial investment" to conserve its donor prospect management resources (Sargeant and Shang 2017, 81). With competing forces of both time and limited resources, a nonprofit must be strategic in its fundraising efforts and focus its philanthropic energies.

As part of donor research, wealth screening reviews "real estate ownership, business affiliations, and stock holdings in public companies" (donorsearch.net n.d.). These reviews of individuals can support the funding options for a person, couple, or family and can help ensure a nonprofit asks for enough and do not leave funds "on the table." The goal is to make a target ask that is an appropriate match between the nonprofit, the person, and the situation. An organization can then target its fundraising lists in order to focus time and energy. In 2021, companies like Wealth Engine, iWave, Blackbaud, and EverTrue can screen against donor lists or donor databases. The American Prospect Research Association maintains ethics and standards on how to manage wealth screening (aprahome.org 2022).

Engagement

Engagement is also important to consider. This level of involvement can be paired with donations and volunteerism number of events, frequency, type of volunteer engagement, board involvement, among other factors.

Data Analytics

Data analytics enable a nonprofit to be more efficient in their fundraising efforts by assessing donor behavior (Nandeshwar and Devine 2018, Chapter 4). From short-term planning to long-term strategy, data analytics can help an organization make decisions and support an organization in its work. One way is through using Rosso's "concentric circles" model, a framework to help determine the best prospects or supporters for a nonprofit. Named for Henry Rosso, who is often referred to as the founder of fundraising, this model places top donors into the inner giving circle of the nonprofit (Grant Adviser 2009). By identifying donors "closer" to the nonprofit that are more likely to give in larger amounts, a nonprofit can determine where to focus its fundraising efforts. Donor modeling can also be used to create top donor prospects for move management or identifying prospects in the database who can be converted into donors (Pelletier 2016, 87).

When considering donor modeling, the nonprofit needs to be sure they can make something useful come from it. Some industry experts call such processes "True but Useless," so all the data that a nonprofit can gather still needs to have value (MacLaughlin 2016, 16). When it comes to limited resources, another important factor that nonprofits need to consider is predictive modeling. In other words, what fundraising strategies have a "higher likelihood to engage, donate, lapse or renew their support" (MacLaughlin 2016, 30). Factors such as previous support, attending events, previous or current board engagement, or simply having been part of the cause can help support predictive modeling. These "descriptive analytics" can help support the cause or output from an appeal or event (MacLaughlin 2016, 37).

In short, nonprofits can be better prepared for their future and organizations can continue to support their missions by understanding future trends in fundraising. And that future includes millennials. Nonprofit organizations have substantial work to do to tap into millennial giving. Millennials spent $1.2 *trillion* in 2020 (Netzer 2020). How can nonprofits direct some of these funds toward philanthropy? As the current largest generational group in the United States, millennials have the greatest potential for giving and volunteering (Hartman and McCambridge 2011; Milliron 2008; Gorczyca and Hartman 2017, 416). The next chapters look more closely at the phenomenon of millennial giving.

References

"A History of Modern Philanthropy: 1930–1980." 2022. Accessed November 26, 2022. https://www.historyofgiving.org/.

"About the Giving Pledge." n.d. Accessed October 1, 2022. https://www.givingpledge.org/about.

"American Religion Timelines." n.d. Accessed December 15, 2022. https://thearda.com/us-religion/history/timelines?tid=10&tab=2.

"Annual Fund Giving Societies." n.d. Accessed December 17, 2022. https://www.rhodes.edu/alumni-development/ways-give/annual-fund-giving-societies.

aprahome.org. n.d. Accessed November 1, 2022.

Birkholz, Joshua M. 2020. *Fundraising Analytics: Using Data to Guide Strategy*. John Wiley & Sons.

Bremner, Robert Hamlett. 1988. *American Philanthropy*. University of Chicago Press.

Candid. July 17, 2001. "Independent Sector Reports Number of Charities Increased Dramatically in 1990s." Accessed December 18, 2022. https://philanthropynewsdigest.org/news/independent-sector-reports-number-of-charities-increased-dramatically-in-1990s.

charitynavigator.org. n.d. Accessed November 1, 2022.

"Clara Barton: Visionary Leader and Founder of the American Red Cross." n.d. Accessed December 17, 2022. https://www.redcross.org/about-us/who-we-are/history/clara-barton.html.

Council of Foundations: Family Foundations. n.d. Accessed December 17, 2022. https://cof.org/foundation-type/family-foundations.

"Donor-Advised Funds." n.d. Accessed November 1, 2022. https://www.irs.gov/charities-non-profits/charitable-organizations/donor-advised-funds.

Donorsearch.net. n.d. Accessed November 1, 2022.

Eisen, Ben, and Anne Tergesen. 2021. "Older Americans Stockpiled a Record $35 Trillion: The Time Has Come to Give it Away." Accessed October 16, 2021. https://www.yahoo.com/now/wsj-baby-boomers-stockpiled-almost-160853293.html.

Foster, William, and Gail Fine. 2007. "How Nonprofits Get Really Big." Accessed October 16, 2021. https://ssir.org/articles/entry/how_nonprofits_get_really_big.

Foundation Basics. n.d. Accessed November 1, 2022. https://cof.org/content/foundation-basics.

Friedman, Lawrence J., and Mark D. McGarvie, eds. 2003. *Charity, Philanthropy, and Civility in American History*. Cambridge University Press.

Gaudiani, Claire. 2004. *The Greater Good: How Philanthropy Drives the American Economy and Can Save Capitalism*. Macmillan.

"Giving USA 2018: Americans Gave $410.02 Billion to Charity in 2017, Crossing the $400 Billion Mark for the First Time." June 13, 2018. Accessed November

15, 2022. https://givingusa.org/giving-usa-2018-americans-gave-410-02-billion-to-charity-in-2017-crossing-the-400-billion-mark-for-the-first-time/.

"Giving USA 2019: Americans Gave $427.71 Billion to Charity in 2018 Amid Complex Year for Charitable Giving." June 18, 2019. Accessed November 15, 2022. https://givingusa.org/giving-usa-2019-americans-gave-427-71-billion-to-charity-in-2018-amid-complex-year-for-charitable-giving/.

"Giving USA 2020: Giving USA 2020: Charitable Giving Showed Solid Growth, Climbing to $449.64 Billion in 2019, One of the Highest Years for Giving on Record." June 16, 2020. Accessed December 12, 2022. https://givingusa.org/giving-usa-2020-charitable-giving-showed-solid-growth-climbing-to-449-64-billion-in-2019-one-of-the-highest-years-for-giving-on-record/.

"Giving USA 2021: Total U.S. Charitable Giving Remained Strong in 2021, Reaching $484.85 Billion." June 21, 2022. Accessed December 13, 2022. https://philanthropy.iupui.edu/news-events/news-item/giving-usa:--total-u.s.-charitable-giving-remained-strong-in-2021,-reaching-$484.85-billion.html?id=392#:~:text=Giving%20USA%202022%3A%20The%20Annual,%24466.23%20billion%20contributed%20in%202020.

Gorczyca, Matthew, and Rosanne L. Hartman. 2017. "The New Face of Philanthropy: The Role of Intrinsic Motivation in Millennials' Attitudes and Intent to Donate to Charitable Organizations." *Journal of Nonprofit & Public Sector Marketing* 29, no. 4: 415–33.

Hadenius, Axel. 2015. "A State Out of Sight—Which Became Increasingly Visible." In *American Exceptionalism Revisited*, 17–44. Palgrave Macmillan.

Hartman, Jackie L., and Jim McCambridge. 2011. "Optimizing Millennials' Communication Styles." *Business Communication Quarterly* 74, no. 1: 22–44.

Heldt, Rodrigo, Cleo Schmitt Silveira, and Fernando Bins Luce. 2021. "Predicting Customer Value Per Product: From RFM to RFM/P." *Journal of Business Research* 127: 444–53.

"How Philanthropy Diverts Social Movements." March 13, 2019. Accessed December 17, 2022. https://www.niskanencenter.org/how-philanthropy-diverts-social-movements/.

IRS Charities and Nonprofits A-Z Site Index. n.d. Accessed March 17, 2021. https://www.irs.gov/charities-non-profits/charities-non-profits-a-z-site-index.

Katz, Stanley N., and Benjamin Soskis. 2018. "Looking Back at 50 Years of US Philanthropy." Accessed September 1, 2021. https://hewlett.org/library/looking-back-50-years-u-s-philanthropy/.

Kelly, Jack. 2019. "Millennials Will Become Richest Generation in American History as Baby Boomers Transfer Over Their Wealth." Accessed September 20, 2021. https://www.forbes.com/sites/jackkelly/2019/10/26/millennials-will-become-richest-generation-in-American-history-as-baby-boomers-transfer-over-their-wealth/?sh=254cfab26c4b.

Levitz, Eric. 2021. "Will the Great Wealth Transfer' Trigger a Millennial Civil War?" Accessed September 1, 2021. *New York Magazine*.

Lipset, Seymour Martin. 1996. *American Exceptionalism: A Double-Edged Sword.* WW Norton & Company.

Lipset, Seymour Martin, and Gary Marks. 2000. *It Didn't Happen Here: Why Socialism Failed in the United States.* WW Norton & Company.

MacLaughlin, Steve. 2016. *Data Driven Nonprofits.* Saltire Press.

Milliron, Valerie C. 2008. "Exploring Millennial Student Values and Societal Trends: Accounting Course Selection Preferences." *Issues in Accounting Education* 23, no. 3: 405–19.

Nandeshwar, Ashutosh R., and Rodger Devine. 2018. *Data Science for Fundraising: Build Data-Driven Solutions Using R.* Data Insight Partners LLC.

Netzer, Jaime. July 1, 2020. "The Top Millennial Buying Habits and Insights for 2021." Accessed July 10, 2021. Retrieved from https://khoros.com/blog/millennial-buying-habits.

2020 Nonprofit Employment Report, John Hopkins Center for Civil Society Studies. June 2020. Accessed March 15, 2021. http://ccss.jhu.edu/wp-content/uploads/downloads/2020/06/2020-Nonprofit-Employment-Report_FINAL_6.2020.pdf.

"Other Tax-Exempt Organizations." 2022. Accessed December 25, 2022. https://www.irs.gov/charities-non-profits/other-tax-exempt-organizations.

Pelletier, Marianne. 2016. *Building Your Analytics Shop: A Workbook for Nonprofits.* Staupell Analytics Group.

Raab, Earl, and Seymour Martin Lipset. 1995. *Jews and the New American Scene.* Harvard University Press.

"Recurring Gifts: The Key to Sustainability." 2021. Accessed October 1, 2021. https://www.networkforgood.com/resource/recurring-gifts-the-key-to-sustainability/

"Recurring Membership Fees." 2021. Accessed October 1, 2021. https://gethelp.wildapricot.com/en/articles/82-recurring-membership-fees.

Regents' Rules and Regulations: Rules 60101 Acceptance and Administration of Gifts. December 10, 2004. Retrieved November 1, 2021. https://utsystem.edu/board-of-regents/rules/60101-acceptance-and-administration-of-gifts.

Renz, David O., and Robert D. Herman. 2010. *The Jossey-Bass Handbook of Nonprofit Leadership and Management.* 3rd ed. John Wiley & Sons.

Sargeant, Adrian. 2005. "Church and Parachurch Fundraising in the United States: What Can We Learn?" *International Journal of Nonprofit and Voluntary Sector Marketing* 10, no. 3: 133–36.

Sargeant, Adrian, and Jen Shang. 2010. *Fundraising Principles and Practice.* Jossey-Bass.

Sargeant, Adrian, and Jen Shang. 2017. *Fundraising Principles and Practice.* 2nd edn. Wiley.

SOI Tax Stats. 2022. Retrieved December 29, 2022. https://www.irs.gov/statistics/soi-tax-stats-charities-and-other-tax-exempt-organizations-statistics.

TED Economics Daily: *Nonprofits Account for 12.3 Million Jobs, 10.2 Percent of Private Sector Employment, in 2016.* August 31, 2018. Accessed November 31,

2022. https://www.bls.gov/opub/ted/2018/nonprofits-account-for-12-3-million-jobs-10-2-percent-of-private-sector-employment-in-2016.htm.

Tempel, Eugene R., Timothy L. Seiler, and Dwight Burlingame. 2016. *Achieving Excellence in Fundraising*. 4th ed. Wiley.

The Concentric Circles of Prospect Research: Research Begins Close to Home. September 15, 2009. Accessed December 17, 2022. https://www.grantadviser.com/ccresearch.

Tocqueville, Alexis de, and Henry Reeve. 1899. *Democracy in America*. Rev. ed. Colonial Press.

Zunz, Olivier. 2014. *Philanthropy in America*. Princeton University Press.

3

Talking 'Bout My Generation: BvB Millennial Case Study

Back in 2016 when I was working in a neuroscience center at a major aspiring R1 university working as a development officer, I was introduced to an amazing group of millennial women and men called Blondes vs Brunettes (now BvB Dallas). As you know, development professionals work with volunteers and those in leadership. One of my board members who was a Baby Boomer—not a millennial—asked why the organization was even bothering with a millennial group. Little did he know that through my work with the group and their steadfast work, the university would soon have the privilege of receiving a $200,000 check for Alzheimer's research. Ironically, that gift by BvB Dallas didn't just serve as a catalyst for an amazing Alzheimer's research lab but made a huge contribution to the research of a neuroscientist.

On my return to the classroom as a graduate student, BvB Dallas' willingness to work with me and serve as a case study struck me as an important harbinger of the future of philanthropy. Despite widespread skepticism within the fundraising community, I dug in my heels and decided I would prove my generation was worth the time and energy to the nonprofit fundraising space. As an elder millennial and fundraiser myself, I realized that we were a misunderstood generation and wanted to explore not just *if* but *how* millennials give, volunteer, and meaningfully contribute to nonprofits. And so I decided the best place to start was with BvB Dallas. I want to take my readers inside the organization and show what really makes millennials tick when it comes to fundraising and volunteering.

H. Hull Miori, *Millennial Philanthropy*,
https://doi.org/10.1007/978-3-031-30269-5_3

Like all case studies, the findings from this one are limited. For example, this particular case study was set in Dallas and focuses on a single organization and therefore is not a national study (which would have been both costly and time-consuming). However, there are equally some benefits that come from focusing on a group from a city like Dallas. The city is fairly transient, and the members of the organization reflect more of a national mindset than just a regional southern outlook. Although the data was collected as a result of each individual member's association with the organization, the views expressed in the surveys and interviews were based on the outlook of the individual and not espousing the "party line" of the organization (indeed, one of the findings is the importance to millennials of maintaining individuality and not being asked to be a mouthpiece for the organization no matter how much they agree with its end goals). So let's take a closer look at BvB Dallas and its members and learn what we can about millennial fundraising from members of this organization.

About BvB Dallas

BvB Dallas (formerly known as Blondes vs. Brunettes) is a nonprofit organization started in 2008 as a young professionals' fundraising group within the Dallas chapter of the Alzheimer's Association. It is primarily populated by individuals falling within the generational boundaries of millennials and therefore an apt group to study with regard to millennial fundraising. In 2013, the group spun off into its own nonprofit (itself an important event for understanding millennials) but retained the focus on funding Alzheimer's research.

Their annual anchor event each summer centers on "The Game"—a powder-puff football contest that pits the blonde female members of the group playing against the brunette women, with the men traditionally serving as coaches. At its founding, blonde members wore pink shirts and brunettes wore blue shirts, but over time the focus on hair color has waned and been less a determining factor regarding what team a member plays for than whether they can practice on a Wednesday evening or Sunday afternoon (Team Pink vs. Team Blue with a neutral Team Purple) (Fig. 3.1).

The founder of the group was inspired by her grandmother's story of battling Alzheimer's and her grandfather's experience as a caregiver. In 2008, she learned of the "Blondes versus Brunettes" concept from the Houston and DC chapters of the Alzheimer's Association and began the nonprofit in Dallas.

Fig. 3.1 BvB Dallas game day 2021 (Photo Credit: Mat Nelson)

About 75 participants—roughly 50 players and 25 coaches—played against each other in the group's initial year, and by the end of the game day in 2008, they had raised over $67,000. Participation has grown steadily since then, and in 2021, the group membership sat at 126 players and 36 coaches, who combined raised nearly $600,000 during the 2021 football season, culminating with Game Day at the Dallas Cotton Bowl (Fig. 3.2).

Most of the revenue comes from what individual members raise, but BvB Dallas also has corporate sponsors and events outside of Game Day. By 2021 the organization had expanded its fundraising to include an Annual Birdies

Fig. 3.2 Game day (Photo Credit: Mat Nelson)

for BvB Charity Golf Tournament, Super Bowling with BvB, a season "Kick-Off" Party, a BvB Block Party, a BvB Talent Show and Auction, personal participant fundraisers, Words with Friends tournament, give-back shopping events and even virtual happy hours and trivia nights (bvbdallas.org 2021).

Each team member is expected to raise a certain amount of money each year. Initially, the fundraising goal was $750, but by 2021 that number had increased to $1,250. Tellingly, each member is given the freedom to raise money in their own way. Members fundraise in a variety of ways, from hosting happy hours and yoga events, organizing lip sync battles and golf tournaments, promoting March Madness contests, jewelry give-back events, or even parties at their local dog parks—and of course through online fundraising. The organization then uses the money raised to fund local organizations working both in Alzheimer's research and caregiving.

The mandate from both the local Alzheimer's chapter and the national association was that the Blondes vs. Brunettes group divert 40% of gross funds raised to the national office with the remainder going to the local chapter to be distributed by the board of directors. While Alzheimer's disease is an international and national concern, the young women and men of the Blondes vs. Brunettes Dallas chapter of the Alzheimer's Association at the time increasingly wanted to channel their funding locally, and in 2013 exited the national Alzheimer's Association to become BvB Dallas (the name Blondes vs. Brunettes is trademarked by the national Alzheimer's Association).

This desire by millennials to keep funding local is reflected in the literature (Millennial Impact Report 2016). Millennials nationwide are wary of institutions in general—sometimes you even hear them colloquially refer to "the man"—and across America groups with millennial membership are increasingly breaking free from national nonprofits in favor of a more localized funding model (Dunham + Company 2017, 9) (Fig. 3.3).

Roadmap for the Research

To learn more about millennial fundraising, two overarching questions guided the design of the surveys and interviews:

- *What factors influence millennial philanthropy?*
- *How should nonprofits engage with millennials for fundraising?*

Fig. 3.3 After party after the game (Photo Credit: Mat Nelson)

These two questions look at the idea of millennial philanthropy from a two-way lens—both from the individual millennial perspective and from the nonprofit angle. But there was still the issue of how to articulate those questions within interview and survey instruments. When examining BvB Dallas, one immediately notices the unique relationship the members have to the organization, the community, their families, their peers, and even religion. To that end, I consulted and utilized several different frameworks for understanding these interchanges and why millennials give. Three in particular emerged as useful constructs for understanding millennials: social exchange theory, which uses an economic exchange model and conceptualizes a two-way exchange occurring; generational theory, which sees persons uniting together through major events; and warm glow theory, which focuses on the joy of giving. These three theories help frame philanthropy by bringing into sharper relief the relationship between volunteers and a nonprofit, the role generations can play in fundraising, and the sheer joy giving can bring.

Social Exchange Theory

Social exchange theory views giving as a two-way relationship resting on reciprocal exchanges between two groups, individuals, or a combination of the two that "tend to engender feelings of personal obligation, gratitude and trust" (Tsai and Cheng 2012, 1020). Social exchange theory, therefore, looks at fundraising through an economic exchange model lens (Emerson 1976, 335) where a donor gets something like a tax receipt and then the nonprofit receives funding resources or volunteer hours in return. This exchange can be seen in the desire BvB members have to play because they want to help the "cause," which helps others but also helps their future selves (after all, curing or preventing Alzheimer's will help the younger generation) as well as participating in social, networking, or job benefits. Many of the members shared during interviews that the benefits that they receive include "gaining status," "comradery," and "opportunities to give back." Social exchanges occur successfully when persons within an organization feel the organizational environment is fair (Tsai and Cheng 2012, 1020). Those feelings then carry over into the volunteer relationship, which can deepen how the person feels about the organization overall (Trent 2020, 2176).

Generational Theory

Founded by Strauss and Howe, generational theory (as it suggests) views fundraising through the lens of generations (Wilson and Gerber 2008). It sees fundraising as less about the individual's personal inclinations and rather more about the individual's grouping based on age and the major events that defined that generation (Li, Li, and Hudson 2013). This cohort is clumped together because they experienced similar things together during a similar age, and as a result experiences patterns in how they work, play, and interact (Knight 2009, 13). These change for each generation and can even change over time within a generation (Drago 2006). While resting on generalizations that do not apply to every individual, generational theory has been successfully used to understand millennials with respect to work, tourism, military recruiting, and higher education (Wilson and Gerber 2008; Buskirk-Cohen, Duncan, and Levicoff 2016; Thach, Riewe, and Camillo 2020). Interviewees were very aware of being part of a generation but also of the monikers that come attached to it including "entitled" and "lazy" given to them by older generations.

Warm Glow Theory

Warm glow theory sees fundraising through the lens of the "personal satisfaction derived from the act of giving" (Null 2008, 1)—in other words, what donor doesn't love to see their name on the wall, on a building, or associated with a named scholarship? By taking part in an action that is deemed virtuous, each individual is also taking part in something bigger than him or herself (Feddersen and Sandroni 2009). This theory sees giving as "impurely altruistic" (Andreoni 1990) because the giver gets something in return, and therefore, the transaction has its roots in economics. It is similar to social exchange theory; however, instead of a tax write-off, the donor gets in return prestige, rewards from a religious perspective (for good works), or simply the satisfaction of doing good—which causes them to want to donate (Harbaugh 1998). For example, interviewees noted feelings of compassion they had toward those suffering from Alzheimer's but also wanted to be "recognized" for their good deeds. The role of generations in the backdrop can interact with warm glow theory, as when interviewees noted the status and the "big role" they will have moving forward through engaging in nonprofits.

Interview: Tayyab Yunus

Biography

Tayyab Yunus is the founder and principal of Intuitive Solutions, where he currently serves as the Dean of the Intuitive Institute and Chief of Nonprofit Strategy of Intuitive Consulting. He is adjunct faculty at Indiana University's Lilly Family School of Philanthropy, Visiting Faculty at Bayan Graduate School, and the President of the Center on Muslim Philanthropy. He holds an MBA from the University of Illinois Urbana-Champaign and is a candidate for a Doctorate in Business Administration at Walden University (2023). Fueled by his life mission to improve the human condition, Tayyab has been providing strategic guidance to both profit and non-profit organizations for over 20 years.

What is Your First Memory of Philanthropy?

My parents used to take us to Pakistan every summer. There they would be met by poor families, widows, orphans, etc., who would come to see them. I would watch them give. In the states, they would support nonprofits.

What is Your family's Influence on Philanthropy?

Dad was one of the founders of the largest American Muslim nonprofit in the United States, the Islamic Circle of North America. He was President for 17 years. He supported the establishment of mosques and schools across America. My mom, with a 10th-grade education, engaged in local philanthropy supporting poor families in the small town of Bonifay, Florida, where we lived. I have seven siblings. All eight of us are engaged in philanthropy, both establishing and leading organizations, as well as donating significant amounts.

What is the Last Gift You Made and Why?

My giving is continuous. Most of my giving is to support salaries for heroes/sheroes who are trying to quit their job to start a nonprofit or for-profit social enterprise to fulfill their philanthropic dream. That results in about $500,000 per year. My largest gift directly to a nonprofit this year was $35,000 for capacity building in the form of training, education, and professional development. It resulted in over 700 people trained in global fundraising and development.

What Has Been Your Favorite Gift?

My favorite gift has been the ones made in private that no one knows about, not even my family. Specifically to orphans and widows in South America and Africa.

How Did You Get Involved with the Nonprofits You Are Involved in?

I am always involved. My life is centered around philanthropy. My involvement stems from my friends, family, work, mosque, and networking group.

How Many Nonprofits Are You Engaged in?

100+

How Did You Get Involved?

At 17, I was a co-founder of a nonprofit. Since then, I've never left philanthropy.

Do You Raise Funds for These Nonprofits, Give Personally, or Both?

Both.

What is Your generation's Biggest Influence in Philanthropy?

Carrying out philanthropy that we learned from our parents—that and trying to pass it on to our children.

What Do You Hope for Your Generation?

That we become the largest impact on philanthropy ever, and that we are able to truly display empathy and pass it on to the next generation.

Data Collection

This study was conducted via two sets of interviews. I was introduced to the organization and interviewees and was grateful to the organization and members for offering to be interviewed more than once. The first wave took place in the summer of 2017 and twenty-five members of the group responded affirmatively to an invitational email (i.e., convenience sampling). Interviews lasted between thirty minutes and one hour and took place at BvB Dallas practices. Two of the interviewees were non-millennials and were not included in the broader millennial data; however, their commentary was included to show how membership feels about millennials (and they had a lot to say!). Interview participants were asked a wide range of questions about themselves, views about their role in BvB Dallas, their philanthropic behavior, perceptions about millennials, and responses to COVID-19. Sample questions included "In your opinion, does the organization, host any events that cater to the millennial generation? If yes, what type of events do you host?" and "Which social media platforms do you use?".

During the 2021 follow-up, seven interviews were conducted with members of the board of directors. Interviewing the board of directors offered the opportunity to refresh the data in particular in light of the pandemic and the Black Lives Matter movement, and additional questions were added about both. Although smaller in number, these interview responses revealed a saturated (i.e., similar) set of information (and the same was true in the 2017 interviews), offering some confidence regarding the findings as not reflecting the opinions of outliers. Interviews lasted between thirty minutes and one hour and took place online (due to the pandemic). Six of the seven were millennials and the remaining interviewee was Generation X.[1] As a fundraiser in the local community, I also kept up with information about their events, personally attended their gatherings, as well as followed them on social media handles and their website.

The full protocol for both interviews and the survey instrument are included in the Methodological Appendix. To take a deeper dive into millennial behavior, additional questions were asked about race, perceptions of millennial status, ethnicity, income, gender, if the person owns a home, income level, and inheritance from family. The other questions were similar from other previous years (Fig. 3.4).

Millennial Giving and BvB

One can see from Table 3.1 the funding and volunteer trends that emerged when interviewing BvB Dallas. The members consistently volunteer 100 hours of their time while leadership doubles that compared to the 40-hour average reported by Dunham + Co. in 2017. But the BvB group doesn't just volunteer more of their time but also donates at a much higher rate compared to the national average for millennials—two to three times as much depending on which measure you use (Dunham + Company 2017; Millennial Impact Report 2015). The 23 millennial interviewees in 2017 averaged $1,704 in donations across all nonprofit giving in 2016, while the average giving of the second-wave participants in 2021 was $1,050.60. As the board

[1] Because this sample is smaller it is perhaps worth noting additional self-reported demographics: five participants were women and two were men. Six participants identified as white and non-Hispanic and one member identified as Asian. Three participants identified as broadly Christian, one participant identified as Catholic, one participant identified as Jewish, and two participants did not identify with a religion.

Fig. 3.4 Game day 2021 (Photo Credit: Mat Nelson)

gives less than the general membership this may be "substitution theory" at work where time is given more than money.

These millennials don't just volunteer more and donate more than the average millennial; their giving is on par with other generations while their volunteering far outpaces Gen Xers and Boomers alike. While these are just the findings for one group in the Dallas market (which admittedly is a bit better off economically), the members of the group were diverse and like many Dallas residents were transient and came from different demographics.

Table 3.1 Generation giving in comparison to BvB

Generation	Dunham + Co Avg. Giving Per Year	Millennial Impact Report Avg. Giving Per Year	Dunham + Co Avg Vol. Per Year	BvB Results	
				Avg. Personal Giving Per Year	Avg Vol. Per Year
Millennials	$580	$481	40 hours	$1,704 (2017) $1,050 (2021)	100 hours (members); 200 hours (leadership)
Gen X	$799	$1212	34 hours		
Boomers	$1365	$732	41 hours		
Matures	$1,093	–	70 hours		

(Dunham + Co 2017; Millennial Impact Report 2015; BvB Interviews 2017 and 2021).

Some told stories of being first-generation college students or dual-race whereas others were executives at large companies. Many said they were the first members of their families to actively engage in being philanthropic. Regardless of the diversity of the backgrounds of the millennial members of BvB Dallas, the main takeaway from this data is clear: if you can get them to donate their time, you can get their personal dollars (and in this instance their personal donation (not what they are getting from others) was significantly *more* than their counterpart generations).

Factors Influencing Millennial Giving

Philanthropic behavior is a large part of this generation. Observations from 2017 interviews talked about millennial BvB members with enthusiasm and what can be described as intense pride. While following this group what was particularly striking was how quickly their attitudes toward technology changed: "Tiktok is the best" to "Tiktok is dead," and "I am only on Facebook to fundraise" to "I am on Facebook to fundraise from my parents' friends." But other attitudes stayed steady, allowing for some deeper insights into how BvB generates those impressive numbers among its millennial members—and how your nonprofit can too. When analyzing the interviews, I identified six unique themes that played an outsize role in giving by members of the millennial generation: religion, social justice, family, friends and peers, proximity, and flexibility.

Religion

Millennials are less religious but tend to view themselves as spiritual (King 2016, 7). Did this generation lose religion? In the first set of interviews from 2017, only one interviewee out of 23 noted church or place of worship attendance and no one mentioned a specific religious organization they gave to. The interviewees did cite parents and family members giving to religious organizations, including the Jewish Federation, Buckner International, and other local faith-based organizations. Members also recalled family experiences with episodic giving and volunteering during the Christian holidays, giving back and volunteering with family at a local church or parachurch organization, and supporting the church through tithing. Clearly, the influence and values were present, but these millennials did not absorb giving around religion.

In the second set of interviews, this pattern persisted. That interview added a more explicit question on parental influence and parent's religious affiliation, but neither of these apparently had any influence on the philanthropic behavior of interviewees (e.g., the likelihood of tithing or giving generously to faith-based organizations was not at all influenced by parental patterns of behavior). Only one participant reported that religion played a factor in their giving. He gave to both a church and faith-based organizations, but also identified as a "cusper" and on the edge of being Generation X (as an elder millennial he might also have the ability for more giving capacity). Another participant had a husband who was Catholic so they gave to his faith-based organization.

Religious service attendance is currently the number one indicator of philanthropy for giving as a whole (King 2016, 6). While participation at places of worship and religious organizations continues to decline, it falls off a cliff with the millennial generation—despite the fact that 60% of millennials identify as spiritual (King 2016). This is especially noteworthy because of its potential to impact the future of philanthropy. If the current trends hold, what will organizations do that come from the faith-based backdrop? How will nonprofits engage a generation that no longer attends religious services like previous generations? They will need to speak to other millennial interests if they want to garner their support.

Social Justice

Research shows that millennials are more inclined to give to causes than institutions or brands (Millennial Impact Report: Ten Year Looking Back, 2020). Millennials engage more with social movements that offer a loose but sustained vision rather than responding to the appeals of a single large organization. For example, the nonprofit community saw an increase in philanthropic gifts to organizations like Planned Parenthood Federation, American Civil Liberties Union, National Immigration Law Center, and Southern Poverty Law Center after the 2016 elections and to historically black colleges during the Black Lives Matters movement in 2020–2021 (Fischer 2018; Kaplan 2017; Anderson and Lumpkin 2020). These increases were driven in part by the actions of millennials. And it's also very clear that millennials show up for certain nonprofits and causes. When Roe vs. Wade was overturned, millennials expressed their views through their giving. They also give with every school shooting. Millennials are also more likely to support non-government organizations (NGOs) in developing countries (Martinez 2014). They are giving to causes that matter to their generation and they give with their dollars and their voices—and they are giving more than you think. Some fundraising blogs and academics described this as "angry" fundraising, but clearly falls into the social justice arena.

At the same time, millennials are less likely to give to a cause aligned with an institution than previous generations (Millennial Impact Report 2016). However, if you are with a "big brand nonprofit," don't panic. Millennials don't penalize you automatically. Organizations should focus on the work and the impact they make no matter their size, and consider closely the interests of millennials. Especially if you are a larger nonprofit, millennials will care less about your size than what the organization can do in terms of local support, making a difference, and being genuine in making change happen. The case study interviews reflected this belief in their desire to donate locally and be engaged with "local causes," whether it be Alzheimer's research or "Black Lives Matters." Social justice concerns were even more heightened in the second round of interviews, likely in the wake of the murder of George Floyd. BvB Dallas also went through a period of self-examination and hosted socially distanced town hall events during COVID-19 to discuss how it would respond to the Black Lives Matter movement and social equity concerns in general as an organization. The nonprofit in years prior had changed the team names from Blondes and Brunettes, which had undertones of racial bias (blonde hair being typically reserved for Whites). To eliminate these concerns, the teams now rely on jersey colors, with pink and blue jerseys representing the teams and purple jerseys representing the administrative or fundraising team (admittedly one player recognized the gender bias involved in the color choices but the group wanted to make changes one step at a time). Leadership was even gravitating away from team colors and "day of the week" for practice days.

In sum, millennials are no longer worried about being in the fundraising room; they want a seat at the table and want to know who else will be there too (but they want a selfie first). Tellingly, not a single interview mentioned the work of a big nonprofit or a nonprofit with a recognizable brand. Instead, two of the 2021 interview participants were excited and went to great lengths to share the news of their new beneficiary working on a Alzheimer's grant in underserved racially diverse communities that typically do not have access to medical care. Undoubtedly, they felt strongly about this grant because it was given during a time in the community when significant social equity concerns were being openly discussed. Organizations need to take heed of these changes and begin to learn about social justice, how it is impacting nonprofits, and what they can do to bolster their brand while responding to the desires of millennials.

Family

Family has limited overt influence on millennial giving, with parental influence hovering off-stage in the category of "fond memories." Interviewees only could vaguely remember what their parents and family gave to, with comments ranging from "maybe they gave to healthcare" to "I think they gave to the church but don't know how much." The first wave of interviews revealed that almost half of the participants were aware of their parents' engagement in philanthropy but with no real awareness of the type of gifts, amounts of gifts, the length of the philanthropy, and types of organizations. Comments from the interviews included remembering "receipts in the mail" to helping "through the uncle's church feeding the homeless." For these participants, family appears to have normalized the practice of philanthropy, even if the type of gift or cause is not something that seemed to be a priority. (Remarkably, based on my role in fundraising in the community, I am very aware that some of the interviewees' families are very influential philanthropists within the greater Dallas community and find it fascinating the interviewees were not aware of their family's large-scale contributions to the community.)

This does not mean that family has no role or is excluded from philanthropic activities. While uncertainty reigned with respect to donating money, interviews did reveal that a few participants profoundly felt a strong family influence on volunteerism. They considered volunteerism and in-kind donations as an equally important part of their philanthropy. And certainly that attitude carried over to the actual games the group would host, which were very well attended by friends and extended family who drove for hours or even flew in to attend and who would proudly wear t-shirts and wave signs supporting the cause. The group's leadership confirmed that many of the players invite their family, friends, co-workers, and even childhood neighbors to attend, and BvB alumni attend with their families as well. Members also leverage family connections when it comes to fundraising. For example, one long-term member of BvB reached out to her family members to gain corporate sponsorships, including a luxury car dealership that displayed cars on the field and offered giveaway items in the VIP suite. Another player worked for the Dallas Mavericks and used their corporate connections to bring the Maverick Maniacs for field entertainment as well as asking the Dallas Mavericks announcer to volunteer his time for the game.

Family connections to the cause itself did have a large role in motivating involvement in BvB Dallas. Based on the first wave of interviews, two-thirds of the millennial participants have a family member or friend suffering from

Alzheimer's, which lines up with the information the Co-President shared at the time that approximately 60% of the membership had been personally affected by Alzheimer's (Morgan, Katie. Interviewed in 2017). These statistics align closely with national statistics for participation as being primarily driven by personal experience. Usually, the person was a grandparent or a parent suffering from the early onset of Alzheimer's. At the end of each practice, a team member would tell a personal story on why they are involved in BvB Dallas. The group's website also quotes members saying they are playing for "Grandpa Jim," "Mam-Maw," "Papaw living with Alzheimer's," and "in memory of my grandmother Ruby" (bvbdallas.org/programs 2021). That said, many participants stated that the disease is not just a grandparent's disease or a gray disease, but rather a significant global crisis that needs to be addressed for the "greater good" (BvB Dallas interviews 2017 2021). But while the greater good is getting rid of Alzheimer's, the motivation behind it is not purely altruistic but rather a form of social exchange regarding their volunteerism and/or giving—because helping their family and friends also means getting rid of the disease before they reach the age where they can develop it. These personal stories about Alzheimer's don't just provide an understanding of why these millennials are involved with BvB Dallas but the new role family plays for millennials in fundraising. Nonprofits need to understand this in order to engage millennials as the "passing of the traditional philanthropic torch" seems to have been extinguished with this generation.

Friends and Peers

Based on interviews, the primary influence for philanthropy comes from friends. The "friend factor" is a powerful force for millennials as friends recruit other millennials to the nonprofit. They are the number one reason a millennial joins BvB—in fact across both waves of interviews, all but three tell the story of being personally invited by a friend: face-to-face, online, or through other social networks. But the influence of friends also explains millennial involvement when there is not a personal connection with Alzheimer's disease—namely the motivation to support a friend. One interviewee became emotional, telling the story of playing for her friends on the team who had been impacted by the disease. Like many friends that were interviewed, she reported that her long-term philanthropic goal was to "kick Alzheimer's ass" (a tagline that comes up quite a bit with this group)—highlighting how the participant's connection went beyond mere friendship to truly embrace the mission of BvB Dallas—and the millennial desire to be part of the "greater good" (FIg. 3.5).

The second wave of interviewees also discussed BvB Dallas as a platform for friendship and social good and how millennials as a generation are "trying to do good" and "really want to get involved in the trenches" with their friends. In the words of one interviewee, it was easy to ask other millennials to join "know[ing] this generation really wants be involved"—not just to support a "best friend's mom with Alzheimer's," but also as a "way to meet new people." Interviews indicated that the nonprofit provided a place to network for jobs or even love matches—all while doing good.

Members of BvB Dallas reported staying connected to the organization for multiple years and how the organization would recruit them into leadership

Fig. 3.5 Game day 2021: Guests cheering on the game (Photo Credit: Mat Nelson)

positions—positions that would be unavailable to them in larger, more traditional organizations. Indeed, in the first wave of interviews one man and two women discussed an interest in starting their own nonprofit. They did not discuss leadership in the BvB Dallas organization or expanding the mission of the organization. Instead, they expressed interest in serving as the founder of their own nonprofit and demonstrating both the self-serving tendencies of millennials and their entrepreneurial spirit (King 2018).

Recognizing the "social aspect" of BvB for players, coaches, and leadership indicates that millennial actions are not purely altruistic. This is not a bad thing. Like any list of factors one might find regarding why someone gets involved in fundraising, there are many reasons why millennials are motivated. Millennials are not unlike that famous millennial toy—the Rubik's cube. With work, play, friends, networking, love life, and philanthropy no longer in silos, they are a complex puzzle to solve with many moving parts. For millennials they all interconnect, but in new and different combinations than seen in previous generations. To facilitate that, unlike other nonprofits BvB Dallas creates personal connections by offering several opportunities outside the digital world for members to meet face-to-face to fundraise for a cause—being "part of something good"—but also to socialize, network, and provide leadership opportunities (language reflecting these priorities was noted in their collateral as well). Most nonprofit organizations are not doing a good job of getting volunteers and potential donors into the fold. The answer lies in the key to BvB's success—the trio of ways to engage this young group of individuals for a philanthropic cause.

Proximity

Interviewees who were most keen on rejecting the philanthropic preferences of their parents differentiated themselves from their parents on the basis of proximity. These participants emphasized their wish to give to local philanthropic efforts and the importance of their peers' opinions. Their friends' preferences regarding local nonprofits and other activities held considerably more sway for these individuals than did parental influence. Even though participants during the second wave of interviews talked about the global nature of the Alzheimer's disease crisis, the group prides itself on funding locally within the greater Dallas area, with interviewees repeatedly voicing the sentiment of "wanting to know where their money is going." At the same time, they also expressed a lack of trust toward larger institutions: This included not only the national Alzheimer's Association but other national organizations like Susan G. Komen and even giving money to universities. These attitudes make the organization's exit in 2013 from the national Alzheimer's Association to ensure that their funding was used for local initiatives and communities almost feel inevitable. Indeed, across both sets of interviews, only one individual admitted to volunteering for a national organization. This doesn't mean they won't give to the brand, but rather see themselves just simply giving to the cause.

But that didn't exhaust the extent to which millennials valued keeping fundraising local. Participants additionally appreciated the ability to receive feedback from those they support. The members often hear directly from the grant recipients, including researchers and caregiving organizations aligned with the BvB mission. The "warm glow" effect was present in interview answers regarding this topic, as millennials feel emotional rewards by keeping funding local by being part of the solution "in their own backyard" (and conversely distrust national organizations as a result of no parallel feeling to these groups). Transparency was also championed as being understood on the local level. The millennial can feel the emotional rewards of keeping things local—the question then is how does the nonprofit world change its messaging to show return on investment with local impact?

Both/And Not Either/Or

The members of BvB volunteer a lot of their time, ranging from 100 hours for general members and to up to 200 hours for those in leadership positions. This volunteer manpower creates an additional $400,000 of value on top of the cash raised by BvB Dallas (Hrywna 2021). Compared to the national average, the BvB Dallas members volunteer at a significantly higher rate than the average millennial volunteers. But perhaps this isn't surprising given their fundraising above the norm as well, since the correlation between volunteerism and philanthropic giving is well documented (Millennial Impact Report 2015). Studies have shown that donors—but especially millennials—are more likely to donate to organizations they support through volunteerism ("4 Effective Ways to Get Millennials Involved in Volunteering" 2017).

This is the exact opposite of what substitution theory predicts—that persons giving their time do so instead of money. Instead, we see millennials giving money *and* their time. In fact, during interviews further confirmation of this unexpected behavior repeatedly came up: The players did not see their time spent fundraising as part of their volunteer service. In other words, members do not see fundraising as an act of volunteer time, so volunteer hours are probably underreported. They instead see their fundraising as

Fig. 3.6 Game day pre-game 2021 (Photo Credit: Mat Nelson)

"part of the job," especially as it is clearly outlined as part of the "pay for play" expectations for Game Day—reflecting the influence of social exchange theory. Millennials want to know where their money is going, but they also want to volunteer where their money is going. In other words, the millennials want to put their hands on the project and also give there too. Millennials are, therefore, more likely to make a gift if they have an opportunity to volunteer because they see volunteerism and gift-giving as social exchange.

Nonprofits have yet to truly maximize all that millennials can offer philanthropically—if they are willing to adapt their thinking to address these factors (Fig. 3.6).

References

"4 Effective Ways to Get Millennials Involved in Volunteering." 2017. Accessed August 28, 2021. https://thomasfoundation.org/4-effective-ways-to-get-millennials-involved-in-volunteering/.

Anderson, Nick, and Lauren Lumpkin. December 23, 2020. "'Transformational': MacKenzie Scott's Gifts to HBCUs, Other Colleges Surpass $800 Million." https://www.washingtonpost.com/local/education/ackenzie-scott-hbcu-donations/2020/12/17/0ce9ef5a-406f-11eb-8db8–395dedaaa036story.html.

Andreoni, James. 1990. Impure Altruism and Donations to Public Goods: A Theory of Warm-Glow Giving. *The Economic Journal* 100, no. 401: 464–77.

Buskirk-Cohen, Allison A., Tisha A. Duncan, and Margaret Levicoff. 2016. Using Generational Theory to Rethink Teaching in Higher Education. *Teaching in Higher Education* 21, no. 1: 25–36.

bvbdallas.org. 2021. Accessed November 1, 2021.

Drago, James P. 2006. *Generational Theory: Implications for Recruiting the Millennials*. Army War Carlisle Barracks.

Dunham + Company. 2017. "Millennial Donors: They're Not Who You Think They Are." Accessed May 30, 2017. https://www.dunhamandcompany.com/.

Emerson, Richard M. 1976. Social Exchange Theory. *Annual Review of Sociology* 2: 335–62.

Feddersen, Timothy, and Alvaro Sandroni. 2009. *The Foundations of Warm-Glow Theory*. Working paper.

Fischer, Michael. 2018. "Women Drove 'Rage Giving' After 2016 Election: Study." Accessed August 28, 2021. https://www.thinkadvisor.com/2018/10/12/women-drove-rage-giving-after-2016-election-study/.

Harbaugh, William T. 1998. What Do Donations Buy?: A Model of Philanthropy Based on Prestige and Warm Glow. *Journal of Public Economics* 67, no. 2: 269–84.

Hrywna, Mark. April 20, 2021. "Independent Sector Releases New Value of Time of $28.54 Per Hour. Accessed December 20, 2022. https://www.thenonprofittimes.com/news/value-of-volunteer-hour-tops-28/.

Kaplan, Larry. 2017. "How Far Does the Post-election Nonprofit Giving Surge Extend?" Accessed July 11, 2021. https://nonprofitquarterly.org/nonprofit-giving-surge-extend/.

King, David P. 2016. "Millennials, Faith and Philanthropy: Who Will be Transformed?," *Bridge/work* 1, no. 1: 1–10.

King, David P. 2018. "Values and Giving." Dallas-Fort Worth Association of Fundraising Conference, Irving, TX, June 15, 2018.

Knight, Yolande. 2009. Talkin' 'bout My Generation: A Brief Introduction to Generational Theory. *Planet* 21, no. 1: 13–15.

Li, Xiangping, Xiang Robert Li, and Simon Hudson. 2013. "The Application of Generational Theory to Tourism Consumer Behavior: An American Perspective." *Tourism Management* 37: 147–64.

Martinez, Shandra. 2014. "Philanthropy Expert: How you Give Depends on Your Age and Other Donating Trends." Accessed on July 10, 2017. http://www.mlive.com/business/westmichigan/index.ssf/2014/06/philanthropy_expert_how_you_gi.html.

Millennial Impact Report. 2015. Accessed May 30, 2017. http://www.themillennialimpact.com/past-research.

Millennial Impact Report. 2016. Accessed May 30, 2017. http://www.themillennialimpact.com/past-research.

Millennial Impact Report: 10 Years Looking Back. 2020. Accessed May 30, 2017. http://www.themillennialimpact.com/latest-research.

Null, Claire. December 2008. "Warm Glow, Information, and Inefficient Charitable Giving."Accessed August 9, 2021. http://www.sscnet.ucla.edu/polisci/wgape/papers/15_Null.pdf.

Thach, Liz, Sam Riewe, and Angelo Camillo. 2020. "Generational Cohort Theory and Wine: Analyzing How Gen Z Differs from Other American Wine Consuming Generations." *International Journal of Wine Business Research* 33, no. 1: 1–27.

Trent, Sheridan B. 2020. "Communicating Our Way to Engaged Volunteers: A Mediated Process Model of Volunteer Communication, Engagement, and Commitment." *Journal of Community Psychology* 48, no. 7: 2174–190.

Tsai, Ming-Tien, and Nai-Chang. Cheng. 2012. "Understanding knowledge sharing between IT professionals–an integration of social cognitive and social exchange theory." *Behaviour & Information Technology* 31, no. 11: 1069–80.

Wilson, Michael, and Leslie E. Gerber. 2008. "How Generational Theory Can Improve Teaching: Strategies for Working With the Millennials." *Currents in Teaching and Learning* 1, no. 1: 29–44.

4

Time Is Money: GRACE Millennial Case Study

Back in 2006–2007, I was working on my master's thesis in theology, where I was looking for case studies in faith-based organizations. I had the opportunity to meet Grapevine Relief and Community Exchange Agency, now called GRACE. The newly minted CEO Shonda Shaefer had a heart for the mission and a vision for the needs of a growing community near a major international airport. Fast forward to my master's in public affairs and then Ph.D. in public affairs, and Ms. Shaffer and GRACE have continued to be an amazing partner and an amazing organization. In full disclosure, I now live in the community and interact with the organization on a regular basis through other organizations (fundraising association, parent's organizations, woman's club). The organization has grown quickly and is in a large and growing robust city that is attractive to millennials.

Based on my knowledge and history knowing the organization, I was curious about the role of millennials in GRACE. The opportunity to have a partnering quantitative study after the BvB qualitative study was a fun and exciting opportunity to pursue. Plus the BvB study shared the role of millennials and volunteers, but a quantitative study was needed to shed more light on volunteerism and philanthropy. With lessons learned from the BvB study about volunteerism and no mixed methods studies currently in the research market, GRACE offered the perfect opportunity for a case study.

Just as was the case with BvB, this case study of GRACE has limitations. This study comes from a single source as well, which obviously limits its generalizability. It was set in Grapevine, TX, a community whose members

H. Hull Miori, *Millennial Philanthropy*,
https://doi.org/10.1007/978-3-031-30269-5_4

have a strong economic background and unemployment is low (Community Profile 2022). Per the most recent annual report from Grapevine Economic Development Office, the city has 51,470, with 32,141 in the labor force with a 3.01% unemployment rate (Community Profile 2022). Of these residents, 18.3% make $100,000 or more and 6.25% of residents make $75,000–99,999. That said, it is also likely that volunteerism correlates to being economically secure such that you have spare time to give versus having to hold down a second job. As you'll learn below, GRACE is also a faith-based nonprofit within the parachurch category, so the findings might be more applicable to those groups. We also don't know if the individuals involved came from a faith-based background or not, and so their motivations for volunteering are challenging to untangle (i.e., did the volunteers come to the organization through their place of worship or congregation, the local school district were they recruited through GRACE's weekly newsletter, website, or social media advertising?). A smaller study of GRACE was done to shed light on those who do come to the organization from faith-based organizations. Faith volunteerism would be a useful focus for future studies, as would finding a parachurch focusing on social services in a different city to compare to the findings in this study. Nevertheless, despite these limitations there's much to glean from the volunteers at GRACE, so let's dig in and take a closer look at this organization and millennial volunteering.

About GRACE

Originally formed by a conglomerate of five local churches,[1] GRACE was created to address the food pantry services desert after the creation of the Dallas-Fort Worth (later DFW) Airport in 1974. With major cities nearly 20 miles away, the community of Grapevine did not have a cohort of services nearby to respond to the rapid growth of the area. As a volunteer organization started by the Ministerial Alliance to provide a more coordinated response to community needs, GRACE opened its doors on September 13, 1987, with a seed grant of $2,000. Its website spells out its mission clearly:

[1] Churches involved in the initial start-up included First Baptist Church of Grapevine, First Methodist Church of Grapevine, Living Word Lutheran Church of Grapevine, Christ our King Church of Southlake, and St. Francis Catholic Church.

> As a steward of God's blessings and resources in the community, GRACE demonstrates compassion for those less fortunate by providing assistance to individuals and families in crisis and guidance toward self-sufficiency. ("Volunteer Opportunities" 2021)

Per GRACE's website, the original relationship with the five churches has grown to include more than 30 Protestant and Catholic churches (GRACE Website 2021). Donors have also expanded to include a local mosque and synagogue (GRACE Website 2021; GRACE Annual Report 2018, 2019). Today, GRACE is a $7 million organization and multi-service nonprofit which includes services spanning emergency assistance, a community health clinic, transitional housing, seasonal programs, resale stores, and donation centers. Per its 2018 IRS 990 form, GRACE has 86 employees, 24 voting board members, and almost 3,000 volunteers. To fulfill their mission, the staff and volunteers work across four storefronts (a donation station, two resale stores, and one upscale clothing resale store) and one office, and also at the time of the study out of a temporary location that housed the medical clinic and food pantry together. GRACE's resale stores are open to the public and also provide clients with clothing, furniture, and miscellaneous housing items (GRACE Annual Report 2018) (Fig. 4.1).

Many human service organizations receive as much as 40% of their budgets through government funding (Coletti 2018). However, GRACE does not receive any government funding and instead chooses to rely on fundraising and the community (GRACE 990 2018, 2019). Special events include a signature gala, a golf tournament, a dine-around event, and a poker event. GRACE's philanthropic giving includes contributions (24%), special

Fig. 4.1 Food pantry (Photo Credit: GRACE)

events (11%), grants (15%), donated goods and services (26%), donated use of facilities (1%), income from resale stores (22%), and other income (1%) (GRACE Annual Report 2020).

GRACE can also be categorized as a "parachurch." Parachurches are faith-based organizations that" exists alongside the "para" church" (Hammett 1991, 3). Over the past two decades years, faith-based organizations have undergone a shift of cutting programs and rationing services which included stricter parameters and creating revenue by charging fees (Alexander 1999, 63). At the same time, congregations have shifted to primarily do their community work and reach outside their four walls through parachurches (Ammerman 2002; Fitch 2007). The most concise and formal definition for a parachurch is "501(c)3 public charities focused on providing religious goods and services outside of congregational or denominational sponsorship" (Scheitle 2010, 505). As of 2010, there were 46,881 "parachurch organizations" registered with the IRS, but the total number of organizations operating in this fashion is likely larger (Scheitle 2010, 13). For example, consider a basement food pantry that has existed for years within one congregation, while another congregation provides its food services through a formal and complex external organization that files a 990. Are both parachurches, or only the complex organization that now has an EIN number?

For parachurch organizations, religious channels provide a solid base for funding and volunteer support (Ammerman 2002; Baggett 2002). A parachurch organization allows a donor to express their faith, which can translate to volunteerism as well (Sargeant 2005, 133). Sometimes parachurches have created partnerships involving two or more churches that partner together to provide services outside their congregations as a formal, religious nonprofit. More complex parachurch organizations typically work on large-scale projects with larger footprints. For example, World Vision has grown from a small nonprofit into a $2 billion enterprise that provides disaster relief, water relief, hunger management, international adoptions, and human rights as a global organization (Financial Stewardship: World Vision 2021). The Young Men's Christian Association (YMCA) has a large network of locations all over the world (YMCA: Our History 2021).

Volunteerism

Volunteers are often the backbone of nonprofit organizations. As you are reading this, you may remember volunteering at a food shelter, reading to a small child, ringing a bell for the Salvation Army, or supporting your local congregation. You may help your family support their efforts and not even realize that you are part of volunteerism. But what really is volunteerism?

Volunteerism is "any activity in which time is given freely to benefit another person, group or organization" (Whittaker, McClennan, and Handmer 2015, 360). Volunteers can engage in a variety of ways—alone or in a group, periodically/episodically or regularly, and based on interests, skills, abilities, technology, and/or opportunities. Individuals may learn of the activity from a peer, place of worship, online, workplace, or other means. One study found 42% of respondents volunteer because they are asked to participate ("Entrepreneurs' Philanthropy Across Generational Divides" 2020).

A variety of social, emotional, professional, and altruistic motivations can influence volunteer engagement. Volunteers receive benefits from "warm glow, experience…in future paid work, social benefits of interaction with other individuals in the workplace, free or reduced cost access to the organization's services, and non-monetary recognition" (Renz and Herman 2010, 497). Other benefits can include providing or sharpening skills, opportunities to serve on a committee or board, and networking opportunities. We also know from the literature that volunteerism and faith are correlated (Musick and Wilson 2007, 367). Since volunteering is a way to express one's faith, the person can feel like they can eliminate poverty or participate in other issues of social significance (Denning 2021, 53).

Volunteerism is a form of "social-capital" and can provide real value to a nonprofit organization (Musick and Wilson 2007, 5; Independent Sector 2020). Volunteers support the role of nonprofits through time, monetary value, and supporting the mission of the nonprofits (Rehnborg 2009, 2). The impact of volunteerism is partially evident in IRS Form 990's, which are compliance tax documents annually filed by nonprofits with the Internal Revenue Service. Per the National Council of Nonprofits, volunteer time is not reported as a contribution on the 990, but it can be acknowledged on the form to show the larger picture and provide some texture of the nonprofit (Council of Nonprofits 2022). This aspect is important as nonprofits not only look at monetary impact to persons served like patients, students, or food served, but volunteerism shares the larger narrative of the nonprofits mission.

Undervaluing volunteerism is detrimental to nonprofits since it is often serves as the framework for the organization. But it is also unwise for another reason: research shows a positive relationship between volunteerism and giving (Martinez 2014). In addition, they will also be more likely to donate more than a donor who does not volunteer. One such study found half of volunteers donate 50% more when they give their time ("Time and Money the Role of Volunteering in Philanthropy" 2020). In other words, there is an opportunity to have a relationship with our volunteers that can translate them into becoming donors. As noted above, there are several reasons for why people volunteer, including to be more social, to be part of humanitarian concerns, improve social and work skills, and enhance personal growth (Forbes and Zampelli 2014, 228–29). This motivational list creates an opportunity for nonprofits to engage volunteers as financial donors.

Advantages and Disadvantages of Volunteers

Most nonprofits work with volunteers, and they come with pros and cons. A volunteer can provide great support to an organization, while these same volunteers can be a hindrance.

Advantages	Disadvantages
• Provide cost-effectiveness to nonprofits	• Challenging and time intensive
• Keep programs and services maintained	• Can require significant resources
• Provide an opportunity for "productive aging"	• Volunteer recruitment, background checks, and training as well as screening volunteers
• Fundraisers for the organization	• Risk just like employees (handling money, working with minors)
• Ambassadors for the organization	• May have to be fired or terminated
• Extend social networks	• Must sustain engagement
• Provide acceptance for donors	

Advantages

Volunteers provide a "cost-effectiveness" benefit to nonprofits. Many organizations rely on volunteers to keep their programs and services running. At the same time, volunteerism has been considered a sign of "productive aging," offering volunteers with an opportunity to increase their altruistic behavior (Russell et al. 2019, 116).

Volunteers can become strong fundraisers for nonprofits (Renz and Herman 2010, 756) and have the potential to serve as ambassadors and as an extension of the organization within the greater community. Volunteers may also introduce their social networks to the organization, extending the reach of the nonprofit. And volunteers create the psychological wellbeing that provides self-acceptance and belonging for the donor (Russell et al. 2019, 118).

Disadvantages

As discussed earlier, the need to create a meaningful environment and foster strong volunteer engagement is important. However, volunteer management can be challenging and time intensive (Tempel, Seiler, and Burlingame 2016, 459–60). Similar to a paid position, it is ideal to have a volunteer position description and structured training provided. Nonprofits need to have a positive volunteer culture for their volunteers. A disruptive volunteer can discourage a group of good volunteers and create a perception of mismanagement or reveal the reality of issues within the organization. A mismanaged volunteer can create concerns about the organization within the community.

Volunteer programs can require significant organizational resources (Sargeant and Shang 2017, 505–7, 511–12; Tempel, Seiler, and Burlingame 2016, 462–63). Nonprofits typically engage in volunteer recruitment, background checks, and training as well as screening volunteers for skill-sets and time availability. The availability of volunteer opportunities impacts volunteer retention, which adds to stress on nonprofit resources. Volunteer risk management is another factor that nonprofits must consider when taking on volunteers. Are they worth your time, the risk, and the headache? Risks may include working with minors, the type of work, and access to organizations' monetary funds, and working conditions (e.g., the Habitat for Humanity volunteers typically work outdoors and may operate heavy machinery in their roles). Finally, there are concerns about volunteers who do not do a good job or follow-up on assigned tasks (Klein 2019). The hardest part of working with volunteers may occur when a volunteer has to be fired or terminated (Sargeant and Shang 2017, 509–10). A strong procedural framework can mitigate these negative aspects of volunteerism (Renz and Herman 2010, 655–58).

Once volunteers are onboarded, nonprofits also must engage in volunteer supervision as well as stewardship and recognition activities. Some positions are at the same level of work as professional or paid positions. The organizations have positions that include gala chairs, committee chairs, and building volunteers. Volunteers are not paid and organizations will need to utilize non-monetary incentives to keep volunteers motivated (Mobileservice 2021). And in the wake of COVID-19, virtual volunteering requires organizations to create social activities and to find connections so the volunteer can stay engaged (Mobileservice 2017). Nonprofits must recognize volunteers like donors, volunteers have choices in choosing where to give their time and are competing for the resource of their time.

A nonprofit should, therefore, invest in developing valuable volunteer assignments in order to foster positive volunteer experiences (Tempel, Seiler, and Burlingame 2016, 459–60; Renz and Herman 2010, 755). This investment can produce long-term volunteer support and help lower overall organizational expenses. Organizations should consider how people learn about volunteer opportunities as well. Regardless of size, organizations can scale their volunteer programs to fit their specific areas of need. Faith-based organization can recruit clergy members, while social service organizations can recruit translators, social workers, and accountants. Large organizations can recruit architects, lawyers, fundraisers, and event planners.

Volunteerism in the United States

With 25% of the US population volunteering, the American population is activity participating with the community around them (Volunteering Statistics and Trends for Nonprofits 2021). Volunteerism in the United States is valued at $173 billion (Forbes and Zampelli 2014, 227). According to Volunteering Statistics and Trends for Nonprofits (2021), Americans volunteer for a variety of nonprofits including:

- religious (34.1%)
- educational (26%)
- social service (14.9%)
- health organizations (7.3%)

That said, volunteerism as a whole is declining per the US Bureau Labor of Statistics (Harp, Scherer, Allen 2017, 442), although religious organizations are not always counted when factoring in the decline. This trend is for a variety of reasons: inflation, additional responsibilities, lack of interest, the ability of nonprofits to engage the community, and changes in the wake of COVID-19 have all changed aspects of volunteerism (including the role of virtual volunteering). Poor volunteer management can frustrate volunteers, especially if it prevents them from serving effectively decreasing engagement and creating role ambiguity (Harp, Scherer, Allen 2017, 444). Many nonprofits have not adjusted their volunteer opportunities (or simply could not due to staffing issues or regulations) and as a result have lost contact with key constituencies—including millennials. With more than 1.8 million nonprofits in the United States, philanthropy is also in competition with itself.

Though millennials get the moniker of lazy, they actually are not, and their volunteerism is noteworthy. Each year, the average American millennial donates approximately 40 hours of volunteer time (Dunham + Co. 2017, 8–9). This is considerably less than the Silent Generation (70 hours) but only slightly less than Boomers (41 hours). Per the recent Americorps.gov report, 20.8% of millennials participate in local groups or organizations and 19.5% donate $25 or more to charity ("Volunteering in America: Demographics" 2021). This level of volunteer engagement can be significant to an organization, especially if the organization engages volunteers well. Millennials, in particular, have increased their political engagement post 9/11, especially the microgeneration of elder millennials.

One of the challenges facing nonprofits is in recognizing potential volunteers, and overlooking millennials is a major mistake. But there are other groups being overlooked as well such as corporate volunteers. Many nonprofits do not consider offering volunteer opportunities that can reach beyond individuals to engage businesses, but engaging corporate volunteers can be helpful for both nonprofits and corporations alike. The advantages include employees sharpening their interpersonal and professional skills (Peloza and Hassay 2006, 358) while corporations can provide funding to nonprofits. Contributions of corporate and corporate volunteerism are scarce in the literature, but based on 2001 statistics, US nonprofits can utilize corporate volunteering relationships to gain potential access to $9 billion in philanthropic funding (Peloza and Hassay 2006, 357). And as it turns out, millennials are looking to corporations as an opportunity for access to engage in philanthropy (conscious capitalism, corporations with days off to volunteer, and other engagement with the community) (Miori 2019).

Roadmap for the Research

To learn more about millennial volunteering, two overarching questions guided the analysis of the data:

- *Which generations are most engaged in volunteerism?*
- *Are there activities that impact volunteerism?*

The GRACE Volunteer study falls under two theories in the broader literature on philanthropy and volunteering: social exchange theory and public service motivation. They come from different disciplines: social exchange falls under the study of economics while public service motivation falls under public administration. But they also root the reason for altruistic behavior in two opposite human psychological needs.

Social Exchange Theory

As you will recall from the last chapter, social exchange theory is based on the idea that human behavior is an exchange of activity for rewards and costs (Nunkook and Ramkissoon 2012, 998). The "two parties may generate mutual obligations" in a social exchange (Trent 2020, 2177). Social exchange theory has been used to explain social power, networks, organizational justice, psychological contracts, and leadership (Cropanzano and Mitchell 2005, 874–75). In regards to volunteerism, there is an opportunity for exchange of goods and egoistic nature simultaneously (Phillips 1982, 118). Volunteerism often times comes from a reward system engrained into society often with youth (Corrigan 2001, ii). At the same time, volunteers can be particular in what they select for their activity and this can lead to an exchange that can also lead to pettiness (Kim, Zhang, and Norton 2019, 361).

Public Service Motivation

Public service motivation (PSM) is a sense of duty to support the community, an obligation that comes from the underpinnings of commitment to public service, social justice, compassion, and self-sacrifice (Perry 1996, 5–6). PSM has its roots in research into the workforce but can also be extended to volunteer services. The nonprofit sector works with this level of embeddedness through volunteerism (Ward and Miller-Stevens 2021, 316; Perry and Wise, 1990). Nonprofit leaders, staff, and volunteers have the opportunity to be part of the greater good and serve the public interest (Perry and Wise 1990, 370). Volunteering can indicate a person's commitment to a nonprofit, and public service motivation can be measured in three ways: hours per month, volunteering intensity, and frequency (Costello, Homberg, and Secchi 2020, 990).

Interview: Chris Bean

Biography

Chris is 35 years old and lives in Fishers, Indiana with his wife Abby and his small children Caroline and Henry. They attend St. Luke's United Methodist Church in Indianapolis. Chris works as a National Practice Director at Thrivent. He graduated from Indiana University (IU) with degrees in Finance and Supply Chain Management. He, currently, serves on the board of the IU Student Foundation and the Foundation Board of Goodwill of Central and Southern Indiana.

What Is Your First Memory of Philanthropy?

When I was growing up my mother worked at the local homeless shelter in my hometown. I was able to go with her to work and see the needs of those in our community. She was always lending a hand beyond her work responsibilities, and we actively tried to help the families who came through the shelter by spending time with the children, donating goods and money, and trying to bring joy to their lives while in the shelter.

What Is Your Family's Influence on Philanthropy?

Beyond the experience in the homeless shelter, my family growing up and my wife's family have helped influence our approach to philanthropy. My father regularly volunteered as a Big Brother at Big Brothers/Big Sisters, and he regularly opened our home during the holidays to people from his work that may not have others to spend the holidays with. This impressed upon me the importance of human relationships and that our fellow citizens are our responsibility. I've carried that with me throughout my life. Additionally, I've seen my wife's family's philanthropic nature in their support of the church and helping others receive a quality education. Those endeavors have been a central part of our philanthropic approach to help further the mission of those institutions helping people to make the world a better place.

What Is the Last Gift You Made and Why?

We just wrapped up a multi-year pledge with both the IU Student Foundation and Goodwill of Central and Southern Indiana. We chose to make the pledge after going through a family values exercise in which we established two of our values as Impact and Philanthropy. Then we asked ourselves, if these are our values, are we really living them out every day? We knew we could do more. So we committed ourselves to a multi-year pledge to support these two organizations that are bringing about impactful change to people's lives in our communities.

What Has Been Your Favorite Gift?

There are actually two gifts that come to mind. I remember making my first gift to the IU Student Foundation as a recent graduate, and although the amount was small, it felt good to be the one giving after all I had received from the organization and the wonderful people that are a part of it. The second was this latest pledge we wrapped up with the IU Student Foundation. My wife and I are both passionate about education and leadership, and our gift will help them to build out the leadership development program of the Student Foundation. We hope it will help to shape the next generation of leaders and philanthropists in our communities.

How Did You Get Involved with the Nonprofits You Are Involved In?

My family, work, and my personal experiences with nonprofit organizations.

How Many Nonprofits Are You Engaged In?

I am currently engaged in regularly supporting four nonprofits—IU Student Foundation, Goodwill of Central and Southern Indiana, St. Luke's United Methodist Church and Big Brothers Big Sisters of Central Indiana.

How Did You Get Involved?

My wife and I both worked for the IU Student Foundation when we were in college. As the student arm of the IU Foundation, it really shaped our viewpoints around philanthropy. Since graduating from college, it has been a mainstay of our philanthropic support including giving, volunteering, and board service. Along with a handful of other people, I helped found the Young Leaders Board of Goodwill of Central and Southern Indiana. It is a privilege to see how successful and impactful that board has been in its 8+ year existence, including living beyond all the founding members. It has also led to an opportunity for me to serve in a new capacity as a board member of the Foundation Board for Goodwill of Central and Southern Indiana. St. Luke's United Methodist Church is our church, and we are always inspired by the tremendous impact it drives in our greater Indianapolis community and across the world. My wife worked at Big Brothers Big Sisters of Central Indiana, and we have remained supporters of the organization for years. I was also really inspired by the work of the organization when my father volunteered as a Big when I was a child.

Do You Raise Funds for These Nonprofits, Give Personally, or Both?

We do both for some of these organizations and give personally to others.

What Is Your Generation's Biggest Influence in Philanthropy?

I believe our biggest influence on philanthropy is the engagement aspect of our giving. In the past, it seemed like people were happy to give some money to an organization. Our generation is going a layer deeper. We try to understand how organizations work, what kind of impact they have, and I think it is leading to deeper engagement with those organizations beyond monetary gifts to more advocacy, volunteerism, etc.

What Do You Hope for Your Generation?

My hope is that we realize that philanthropy isn't something that can wait until "you've made it." Philanthropy is a lifelong endeavor that we should all be engaged in regardless of how big we think the impact is. Our communities need us now, and we need to be engaged at a level that is meaningful to shape the world we hope to have.

Data Collection and Analysis

A quantitative data analysis was completed from the GRACE database called Abila. The customer relationship management (CRM) software provides a unique opportunity because the organization tracks philanthropic support, volunteerism, and year of birth. Rarely, do researchers get the opportunity to compare these types of data points together. Data periods that were included were from 2015 to 2018.

While maintaining anonymity, the organization provided unique identifiers, constituent type (individuals, corporate, churches, foundations), and birthdays, which enabled the opportunity to assign individuals to generations. The organization also gave the name of the activity the volunteer participated in as well as their start date and end date. The following data was made available: hours, value of the volunteer hour, employer identification, project identification, organization identification, project name, program name, 2018 gift total, 2019 gift total, 2020 gift total, first gift amount, first gift date, largest gift amount, and zip code (Fig. 4.2).

The data included 3,573 observations and 14 variables. To prepare for the coding, the data was cleaned up including navigating duplicates and reshaping the data so that each ID had only one observation per day. To make comparisons easier, aggregates such as variable descriptives were created for the volunteer dataset including annual and total giving figures were created, and additional ID information for volunteers. This allows each observation to retain characteristics like assignments that were unique to the day, but

Fig. 4.2 Graceful Buys (Photo Credit: GRACE)

also will over-represent the annual totals of those individuals who volunteered multiple times in the year since those totals will be attached to multiple observations.

Fifty-two cases had multiple entries for the same day. For those with the same activity, the time was aggregated; for those with different activities in the same day, the amount of time for the full day was aggregated and coded to a new activity "Various" (e.g., someone is both working in the food pantry and in the resale store on the same day). This information was then combined into one data file for the day.

The study uses Ordinary Least Squares (OLS) Regression analysis to understand what factors were associated with the total amount of time spent volunteering in 2018 by a person conducted to analyze GRACE with the 2018 volunteer hours as the reference group (base group for the study). For those unfamiliar with OLS regression analysis, it is a common technique to mathematically describe the relationship between one or more independent quantitative variables and a dependent variable. For example, social scientists are interested in whether women with more educated women have fewer children than women with less education. While no one would expect all women with a college degree to have only one child while women who did not finish high school to have exactly six children, we might expect there to be a linear relationship between the number of years of education and the number of children a woman has. OLS regression analysis allows us to calculate that relationship mathematically when we have data for the number of children and years of education (https://www.encyclopedia.com/ordinary-least-squares-regression).

A generational analysis was completed to look at the volunteer assignments and projects, volunteer hours, volunteer information, and gala attendance. Interactions were created at the 0.05 significance examining the Silent Generation (1927–1945), Baby Boomers (1946–1965), Generation X (1966–1979), and Millennials (1980–1999). All those born in the year 2000 or later were excluded to align with the Internal Review Board (IRB) specifications and exclude minors.

Volunteering and GRACE

The volunteer patterns provide insight into where the volunteers were providing their services and time. Because these patterns were based on quantitative data, they lack information on desires, interest in the organization, and connections to the nonprofit that could help inform some of the patterns.

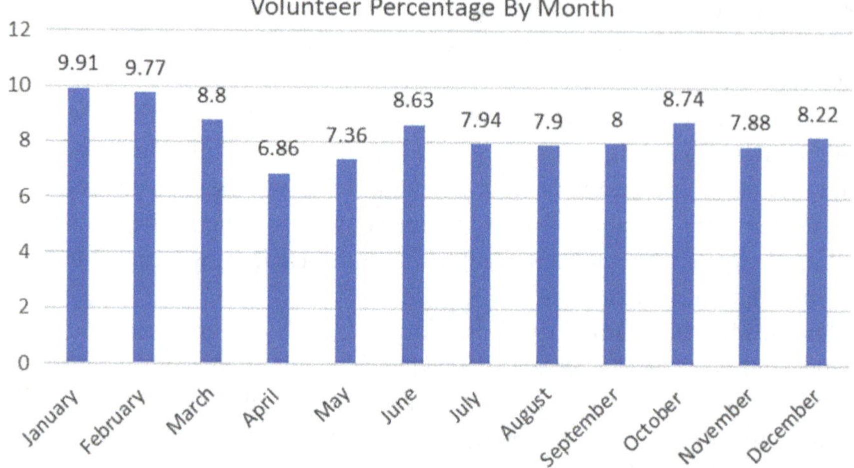

Fig. 4.3 GRACE volunteer percentage by month

The most popular months for volunteering within this dataset are January (9.91%), February (9.77%), and June (8.63%). But why? What can we learn from these patterns? (Fig. 4.3).

A number of factors may contribute to these trends. As one example, each December GRACE hosts the popular annual Christmas Cottage event which "provides new, unwrapped gifts to families facing financial hardship due to limited income or recent emergency" ("Volunteer Opportunities" 2021). It is possible that by attracting people to its services in December that more people become involved in subsequent months. While not the most popular month, the summer month of June is busy as well. The reasoning may be the availability of the summer hours that come from summertime for children and certain employment. Based on the GRACE website, there are some seasonal or episodic activities for summer called "Feed our Kids" that come under the food or pantry services. This event supports the local children and it has Monday-Friday opportunities providing work hours during summer ("Volunteer Opportunities" 2021). In addition, with students out of school, younger volunteers may be available to volunteer or even are trying to fit their volunteer requirements in summertime (Fig. 4.4).

Wednesday is the most popular day to volunteer at 23.5%, followed by Friday at 18.7%, Thursday at 17.9%, and Saturday at 17.9%. Interestingly, weekdays are the most popular time to volunteer, not *weekends* (see Fig. 3.3). By examining the website and volunteer opportunities, it turns out that there are more opportunities available during mid-week than weekends ("Volunteer Opportunities" 2021).

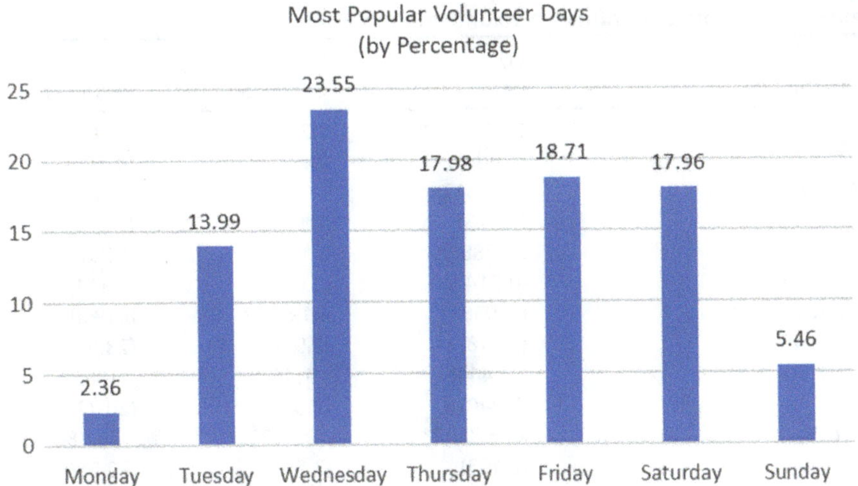

Fig. 4.4 GRACE most popular volunteer days (by percentage)

Factors Influencing Volunteering

Let us look closer at the statistical findings which will allows us to understand better which factors influence volunteering the most. Millennials will serve as the control for the research. In other words, we are comparing all of our data against the main group of our focus group—millennials. Millennials have the moniker of being lazy and uncaring, but this chapter will paint a different landscape. We learn they do volunteer and lean to more social justice activities: feeding the hungry, translating for clients, and work in the medical clinic.

To get into the more technical aspects of the analysis, this study contains three OLS regressions: one with normal standard errors; one with robust standard errors; and one that is adjusted for the clustering that occurs on the ID (see Table 4.1). Though we are concerned with the over-representation of the characteristics of those who volunteer multiple days, the loss of statistical significance on almost all "shared" characteristics may indicate overcompensation. So this study will interpret the OLS regression with robust standard errors. R-square is a goodness-of-fit measure for linear regression model. In this analysis, R-square $= 0.47$, meaning the model explains 47% of the variance in the data.

Table 4.1 Factors that influence volunteering in 2018

Variables	(1) OLS	(2) OLS Robust	(3) OLS Cluster
Volunteer 2017	0.3111***	0.3111***	0.3111**
	(0.008)	(0.032)	(0.146)
Volunteer 2016	−0.0617***	−0.0617	−0.0617
	(0.016)	(0.041)	(0.188)
Volunteer 2015	0.1288***	0.1288***	0.1288
	(0.014)	(0.021)	(0.111)
Silent Generation	6.1938**	6.1938**	6.1938
	(2.818)	(2.910)	(23.551)
Baby Boomer	−1.4445	−1.4445	−1.4445
	(2.440)	(2.555)	(20.729)
Gen X	−26.3802***	−26.3802***	−26.3802
	(2.463)	(2.511)	(20.556)
CSR (Court Service Restitution)	4.5227	4.5227	4.5227
	(14.087)	(5.318)	(16.801)
Client Services	120.3539***	120.3539***	120.3539***
	(6.566)	(4.933)	(30.229)
Clinic	17.5572***	17.5572***	17.5572
	(6.018)	(2.364)	(14.228)
Clothing Room	57.2399***	57.2399***	57.2399***
	(6.608)	(4.092)	(22.152)
Development	31.2563***	31.2563***	31.2563
	(7.469)	(4.258)	(27.051)
Donation Station	14.4986**	14.4986***	14.4986
	(6.180)	(2.061)	(10.728)
Friends & Family (Senior)	24.5926***	24.5926***	24.5926
	(7.718)	(6.787)	(17.435)
Resale	151.9864***	151.9864***	151.9864***
(Euless Graceful Buys)	(6.280)	(4.598)	(40.821)
Resale Main Store	45.5889***	45.5889***	45.5889***
(Grapevine Graceful Buys)	(6.058)	(2.380)	(14.352)
Pantry (Food)	58.0475***	58.0475***	58.0475***
	(5.858)	(2.391)	(15.794)
Seasonal (Holiday)	−10.4891*	−10.4891***	−10.4891
	(6.202)	(1.812)	(7.084)
Special Events (Development)	69.2863***	69.2863***	69.2863**
	(9.599)	(10.947)	(31.585)
Special Projects	0.4744	0.4744	0.4744
	(11.038)	(3.503)	(10.264)
Resale (Euless, Style, and Grace)	85.3493***	85.3493***	85.3493***
	(6.238)	(3.655)	(25.452)
Combination	63.9084***	63.9084***	63.9084***
	(8.902)	(6.887)	(19.896)

(continued)

Table 4.1 (continued)

Variables	(1) OLS	(2) OLS Robust	(3) OLS Cluster
Volunteer Orientation	−1.3256	−1.3256	−1.3256
	(9.281)	(3.680)	(8.590)
Gala 2015	9.9506	9.9506	9.9506
	(11.118)	(8.822)	(19.987)
Gala 2016	−7.4431	−7.4431	−7.4431
	(11.967)	(10.163)	(28.068)
Gala 2017	14.7129***	14.7129***	14.7129
	(4.815)	(3.476)	(19.178)
Constant	21.7083***	21.7083***	21.7083
	(6.198)	(2.846)	(18.374)
Observations	12,862	12,862	12,862
R-squared	0.473	0.473	0.473
Prob > F	0.000	0.000	0.000

Standard errors in parentheses. Robust standard errors in (2) and (3)
Standard errors adjusted for 717 clusters in (3)
***$p < 0.01$, **$p < 0.05$, *$p < 0.1$

The Role of Previous Volunteerism

The OLS analysis found significance in volunteering for future volunteerism. In the nonprofit arena, fundraising has indicators that can help with future philanthropy. For example, a philanthropic gift indicates a greater likelihood of a future gift. As this study confirms, the same holds true for volunteerism. Volunteerism for 2015 and 2017 was positively and significantly associated with 2018 total volunteering ($p < 0.001$) (although the 2016 volunteer year was not significant). In other words, the biggest indicator for future volunteerism was previous volunteerism in two of the years, which aligns with research that shows that one of the biggest predictors of current volunteering and future volunteering is past volunteering (Einolf 2016; Marta et al. 2014). These patterns show attachment to the organization and a desire to stay involved. Given these results, if nonprofits want to increase volunteerism, organizations should consider volunteer patterns in previous years. An interesting but not surprising finding is that the Silent Generation donates the most time. This generation is presumably retired and therefore likely able to donate more time.

These results beg the question of how to get someone to begin to volunteer. The existing literature is weak on how volunteers are recruited whether through recruiting fairs, social media or outside organizations. At GRACE one can see in action the public service motivation theory of serving the greater good by including the wider community through the organization's actions. The desire to ask the volunteer for their time and effort gives them an outlet to give back, serve, and help others.

This information brings up the question for nonprofits about their current recruitment strategies for volunteers. Consider the actions your nonprofit engages in and the communities it serves and whether it appeals to public service motivation or social exchange. Nonprofits cannot ignore current volunteers but engage them successfully for future engagement. Consider how we speak to current volunteers including millennials? We know they engage with their social networks, social justice, and social media. In other words, unlike previous generations they are "socially" connected more than previous generations.

The Role of Generations

There was no significant difference in 2018 volunteering hours for Baby Boomers compared to other volunteer years (2017, 2016, and 2015). However, the Silent Generation were statistically significant with respect to volunteering in the years 2017, 2016, and 2015. To examine the generations deeper, per volunteer the Silent Generation volunteers 6.19 hours more than millennials ($p < 0.001$). Baby Boomers volunteer 1.44 hours less on average than millennials, and Generation X volunteer 26.38 hours less than millennials ($p < 0.001$).

In other words, we can think of the volunteer hours per person like this:

$$\text{Silent Generation} > \text{Millennials} > \text{Generation X} > \text{Baby Boomers}$$

When recruiting volunteers, these generational differences are important to consider. Most nonprofits have limited resources, so when examining who to recruit and who are more likely to be more active volunteers, the organization can create a plan on how to recruit those volunteers based on generation. Though the millennials did not give the most time as volunteers compared to the Silent Generation, they were ahead of Boomers and far ahead of Generation X. Millennials clearly can be valuable volunteers when it comes to the amount of time they give, even if there are fewer of them volunteering in this study than other generations.

This study has the generation donating the largest percentage of volunteer hours as the Baby Boomers, followed by Generation X, then the Silent Generation, and finally Millennials (see Table 4.2).

Table 4.2 Generation count for GRACE data (GRACE 2021)

Generation	Volunteer Hours by Generation	Percentage
Baby Boomer	6,399	49.75
Generation X	3,403	26.46
Silent Generation	2,012	15.64
Millennials	1,048	8.15
Total	12,862	100%

Fig. 4.5 GRACE Gala (Photo Credit: GRACE)

To think about the roles of the millennials, they are 8.5% of the volunteerism in aggregate of the time analysis, with Silent Generation at 15.64%, then Generation X at 26.54% and then Baby Boomers at the most volunteer friendly at 49.75% of the volunteer hours. Based on this case study, millennials volunteered the least number of total volunteer hours, but they still volunteered and in meaningful ways (Fig. 4.5).

The Role of the Gala

Each year GRACE holds a gala—a large-scale fundraising event. Galas are a costly proposition, and organizations should examine whether or not they are effective as fundraising tools but also how they affect volunteering. It turns out GRACE gala volunteerism has a significant impact on future volunteerism with the organization. In other words, the data indicates gala volunteerism influences volunteerism in other areas of the organization. For the 2015 Gala, those that volunteered gave 9.95 more hours of time to the organization than those that did not, while the 2016 Gala led to 7.44 more hours (with p values at 0.259 and 0.464, respectively). The 2017 Gala was statistically significant as well and increased 2018 volunteerism by 14.71 hours with a p value at 0.000. Volunteerism at the gala clearly made a difference for those that volunteered.

The Role of Activities

As a social service agency it is not surprising that GRACE offers several opportunities to volunteer for year-round types of assignments. Many nonprofits do the same. We want to know the impact of these activities on volunteerism from a statistical standpoint; however, in terms of the statistical analysis, several of the assignments had to be combined since the N (the number for the research) was too small and activities were similar in nature to reveal statistically meaningful results on their own.

As activities court service restitution, special projects and volunteer orientation did not reveal any significant relationship to increased volunteerism. Interestingly, these areas were required assignments and so can be intuitively seen as not generating a loyalty factor. But volunteering at the Clothing Room, Graceful Buys Euless (Euless, TX location), Donation Station, Style, and Grace (high-end resale in Grapevine, TX location), and Graceful Buys (Grapevine, TX original location) were positively associated with 2018 volunteering hours ($p < 0.001$). This too is not surprising since these activities offer rewards for volunteers (i.e., social exchange where volunteers can have first access to resale items, opportunities to network, and the ability to get coupons) and more accessible hours (hours available, days opens, skills to sharpen for the volunteer). According to GRACE's annual report, the stores serve as 22% of the annual revenue so the pipeline of a good volunteer stream for these activities is critical to its success (GRACE Annual Report 2020; "Volunteer Opportunities" 2021). Activities such as feeding the community and social service for the community also prove to be statistically significant. Working in a food pantry significantly increases the number of hours one chooses to volunteer by 58 hours (Fig. 4.6).

Fundraising activities are those who volunteer to support fundraising and development events on an as-needed basis. When examining the data, these areas have statistical significance and result in more volunteering hours than the other types of assignments including clinic, medical, senior service, and feeding and the pantry. When looking directly at the impact of the fundraising activities on volunteerism, the special events and development activities both are statistically significant and both have the same p value (p

Fig. 4.6 Graceful Buys (Photo Credit: GRACE)

> 0.000). The coefficient (or the range of volunteer hours) fluctuated from 14.49 volunteer hours to 151.98 volunteer hours. Special events lead to 69.28 hours more volunteering and development 31.25 hours, respectively. These hours support the mission of the organization and its fundraising efforts, and in addition impact volunteerism. In short, volunteers who engage in fundraising activities will volunteer more than those who do not engage in such activities (Table 4.3).

The various volunteer assignments provide insight into volunteerism within GRACE. Two activities fall under social exchange. The resale assignment offers an exchange by giving volunteers access to items that the resale stores sell, a social environment, and opportunities to be involved in a valuable mission. For fundraising, the volunteer gains access to high-profile events and access to community members. But another group of assignments illustrate public service motivation theory in action. The categories include food (including roles within the food pantry), medical care (including roles within the clinic) and senior services. Food, medical care, and senior services volunteer assignments serve the community, and GRACE relies on public service motivation for volunteers for these activities that promote the role of community engagement.

Table 4.3 Activities by theories

	Volunteer activities	Theory	Notes
Resale Shop	Clothing Room, Graceful Buys Euless, Donation Station, Style, and Grace (high-end resale), Graceful Buys (Grapevine, TX)	Social Exchange	Access to social networks, first access to resale items, benefits for discounts
Fundraising	Development; Special Events	Social Exchange	Access to high-end events, "being seen," social networking
Feeding/ Pantry	Food	Public Service Motivation	Greater good, supporting the community, altruism, belief nonprofits can enhance the community
Medical	Clinic	Public Service Motivation	Greater good, supporting the community, altruism, belief nonprofits can enhance the community
Senior Services	Friends and Family Program	Public Service Motivation	Greater good, supporting the community, altruism, belief nonprofits can enhance the community

References

Alexander, Jennifer. 1999. "The Impact of Devolution on Nonprofits." *Nonprofit Management and Leadership* 10, no. 1: 57–70.

Ammerman, Nancy T. 2002. "Connecting Mainline Protestant Churches with Public Life." In *The Quiet Hand of God: Faith-Based Activism and the Public Role of Mainline Protestantism*, edited by R. Wuthnow and J. H. Evans. University of California Press.

Baggett, Jerome P. 2002. "The Irony of Parachurch Organizations: The Case of Habitat for Humanity." *New Directions for Philanthropic Fundraising* 2002, no. 35: 55–78.

Coletti, Joseph. January 8, 2018. "Strengthening Human Services With and Without Government." Accessed December 30, 2022. https://www.johnlocke.org/strengthening-human-services-with-and-without-government/.

"Community Profile." 2022. Accessed December 23, 2022. https://www.choosegrapevinetx.com/site-selection/community-profile.

Corrigan, Michael Wesley. 2001. *Social Exchange Theory, Interpersonal Communication Motives, and Volunteerism: Identifying Motivation to Volunteer and the Rewards and Costs Associated*. West Virginia University.

Costello, Joyce, Fabian Homberg, and Davide Secchi. 2020. "The Public Service Motivated Volunteer: Devoting Time or Effort?" *Nonprofit and Voluntary Sector Quarterly* 49, no. 5: 989–1014.

Cropanzano, Russell, and Marie S. Mitchell. 2005. "Social Exchange Theory: An Interdisciplinary Review." *Journal of Management* 31, no. 6: 874–900.

Denning, Stephanie. 2021. "Persistence in Volunteering: An Affect Theory Approach to Faith-Based Volunteering." *Social & Cultural Geography* 22, no. 6: 807–27.

Dunham + Company. 2017. "Millennial Donors: They're Not Who You Think They Are." Accessed May 30, 2017. https://www.dunhamandcompany.com/.

Einolf, Christopher. 2016. "Millennials and Public Service Motivation: Finding from a Survey of Master's Degree Students." *Public Administration Quarterly* 40, no. 3: 429–57.

"Entrepreneurs' Philanthropy Across Generational Divides." 2020. Accessed August 22, 2021. https://www.fidelitycharitable.org/articles/entrepreneurs-philanthropy-across-generational-divides.html.

Financial Stewardship: World Vision. 2021. Accessed November 1, 2021. https://www.worldvision.org/about-us/financial-accountability-2#1468438377863-040c8abd-5609.

Fitch, David E. 2007. *The Great Giveaway: Reclaiming the Mission of the Church from Big Business, Parachurch Organizations, Psychotherapy, Consumer Capitalism, and Other Modern Maladies*. Baker Books.

Forbes, Kevin F., and Ernest M. Zampelli. 2014. "Volunteerism: The Influences of Social, Religious, and Human Capital." *Nonprofit and Voluntary Sector Quarterly* 43, no. 2: 227–53.

GRACE 990. 2018. Accessed September 27, 2021. https://www.gracegrapevine.org/wp-content/uploads/2021/08/2019-Public-Disclosure-Tax-form-990.pdf.

GRACE 990. 2019. Accessed September 27, 2021. https://www.gracegrapevine.org/wp-content/uploads/2021/08/GRACE-FY20-990.pdf.

"GRACE Annual Report 2018." 2018. Retrieved on September 27, 2021. https://www.gracegrapevine.org/financials/.

"GRACE Annual Report 2019." 2019. Retrieved on September 27, 2021. https://www.gracegrapevine.org/financials/.

"GRACE Annual Report 2020." 2020. Accessed September 27, 2021. https://www.gracegrapevine.org/wp-content/uploads/2021/09/FY2020-Final-Annual-Report.pdf.

GRACE Website. 2021. Accessed October 20, 2021. https://www.gracegrapevine.org/.

Hammett, John Samuel. 1991. *The Southern Baptist Theological Seminary*. ProQuest Dissertations Publishing.

Harp, Elizabeth R., Lisa L. Scherer, and Joseph A. Allen. 2017. "Volunteer Engagement and Retention: Their Relationship to Community Service Self-Efficacy." *Nonprofit and Voluntary Sector Quarterly* 46, no. 2: 442–58.

"Independent Sector". 2020. "Volunteers contribute billions to the United States through their time, talent, and effort in 2020 even while volunteer opportunities were limited due to COVID-19 pandemic." April 20, 2021. Retrieved on August 28, 2021 on https://independentsector.org/news-post/independent-sector-releases-new-value-of-volunteer-time-of-28-54-per-hour/

Kim, Tami, Ting Zhang, and Michael I. Norton. 2019. "Pettiness in Social Exchange." *Journal of Experimental Psychology: General* 148, no. 2: 361.

Klein, Kim. September 18, 2019. "The Pros and Cons of Engaging Volunteers in Fundraising" Retrieved on September 5, 2021. https://fundraisersoftware.com/library/fundraiser-blog/entry/the-pros-and-cons-of.

Marta, Elena, Claudia Manzi, Maura Pozzi, and Vivian Laurance Vignoles. 2014. "Identity and the Theory of Planned Behavior: Predicting Maintenance of Volunteering after Three Years." *The Journal of Social Psychology* 154, no. 3: 198–207.

Martinez, Shandra. 2014. "Philanthropy Expert: How you Give Depends on Your Age and 4 Other Donating Trends." Accessed July 10, 2017. http://www.mlive.com/business/westmichigan/index.ssf/2014/06/philanthropy_expert_how_you_gi.html.

Miori, Holly. 2019. "Conscious Capitalism." American Society Public Administration Conference Presentation.

Musick, Marc A., and John Wilson. 2007. *Volunteers: A Social Profile*. Indiana University Press.

Nunkook, Robin, and Haywantee Ramkissoon. 2012. "Power, Trust, Social Exchange and Community Support." *Annals of Tourism Research* 39, no. 2: 997–1023.

OLS. 2022. Accessed November 1, 2022. https://www.encyclopedia.com/ordinary-least-squares-regression.

Our History. 2021. Accessed October 13, 2021. https://www.ymca.org/who-we-are/our-history.

Peloza, John, and Derek N. Hassay. 2006. "Intra-organizational Volunteerism: Good Soldiers, Good Deeds and Good Politics." *Journal of Business Ethics* 64, no. 4: 357–79.

Perry, James L. 1996. "Measuring Public Service Motivation: An Assessment of Construct Reliability and Validity." *Journal of Public Administration Research and Theory* 6, no. 1: 5–22.

Perry, J. L., & Wise, L. R.1990. "The Motivational Bases of Public Service." *Public Administration Review* 50: 367–73.

Phillips, Michael. 1982. "Motivation and Expectation in Successful Volunteerism." *Journal of Voluntary Action Research* 11, no. 2–3: 118–25.

Rehnborg, Sarah Jane. May 2009. *Strategic Volunteer Engagement: A Guide for Nonprofit and Public Sector Leaders*. RGK Center for Philanthropy and Community Service.

Renz, David O., and Robert D. Herman. 2010. *The Jossey-Bass Handbook of Nonprofit Leadership and Management*. 3rd ed. Wiley.

Russell, Allison R., Ama Nyame-Mensah, Arjen de Wit, and Femida Handy. 2019. "Volunteering and Wellbeing among Ageing Adults: A Longitudinal Analysis." *VOLUNTAS: International Journal of Voluntary and Nonprofit Organizations* 30, no. 1: 115–28.

Sargeant, Adrian. 2005. "Church and Parachurch Fundraising in the United States: What Can We Learn?" *International Journal of Nonprofit and Voluntary Sector Marketing* 10, no. 3: 133–36.

Sargeant, Adrian, and Jen Shang. 2017. *Fundraising Principles and Practice*. 2nd ed. Wiley.

Scheitle, Christopher P. 2010. *Beyond the Congregation: The World of Christian Nonprofits*. Oxford University Press.

Tempel, Eugene R., Timothy L. Seiler, and Dwight Burlingame. 2016. *Achieving Excellence in Fundraising*. 4th ed. Wiley.

"The Pros and Cons of Virtual Volunteering," February 20, 2017. Mobileservice. Accessed September 5, 2021. https://blog.mobileserve.com/the-pros-and-cons-of-virtual-volunteering.

"Time and Money: The Role of Volunteering in Philanthropy." 2020. Accessed October 9, 2021. https://www.fidelitycharitable.org/content/dam/fc-public/docs/insights/volunteering-and-philanthropy.pdf.

Trent, Sheridan B. 2020. "Communicating Our Way to Engaged Volunteers: A Mediated Process Model of Volunteer Communication, Engagement, and Commitment." *Journal of Community Psychology* 48, no. 7: 2174–90.

"Volunteers." 2022. Retrieved on September 27, 2022. National Council of Nonprofits. https://www.councilofnonprofits.org/running-nonprofit/employment-hr/volunteers

"Volunteer Opportunities." 2021. Accessed October 14, 2021. https://www.gracegrapevine.org/get-involved/volunteer/volunteer-opportunities/.

"Volunteering in America: Demographics." 2021. Accessed November 1, 2021. https://americorps.gov/sites/default/files/document/Volunteering_in_America_Demographics_508.pdf.

Ward, Kevin D., and Katrina Miller-Stevens. 2021. "Public Service Motivation Among Nonprofit Board Members and the Influence of Primary Sector of Employment." *Nonprofit and Voluntary Sector Quarterly* 50, no. 2: 312–34.

Whittaker, Joshua, Blythe McLennan, and John Handmer. 2015. "A Review of Informal Volunteerism in Emergencies and Disasters: Definition, Opportunities and Challenges. *International Journal of Disaster Risk Reduction* 13: 358–68.

5

A Look Behind the Numbers: GRACE Millennial Case Study

As explained in greater detail at the beginning of Chapter 4, the parachurch organization GRACE offered the opportunity to perform a quantitative study looking at millennial volunteerism and philanthropy. While Chapter 4 looked more closely at volunteering, this chapter will examine millennial philanthropy quantitatively. The study will look at the motivations for donation decisions by generation and factors influencing donation decisions like volunteerism and gala attendance. The study will also create variables that examine engagement and lifetime giving by generation. The chapter also aims to fill a gap in the literature, which is weak on the role that generation plays in philanthropy (Sargeant and Shang 2010; Millennial Impact Report 2015).

Originally formed by a conglomerate of five local churches,[1] GRACE was created to address the food pantry services desert after the creation of the Dallas-Fort Worth (DFW) Airport in 1974. With major cities nearly 20 miles away, the community of Grapevine did not have a cohort of services nearby to respond to the rapid growth of the area. The group has grown to include more than 30 Protestant and Catholic churches as well as a local mosque and synagogue (GRACE Website 2021; GRACE Annual Report 2020; GRACE 990 2018, 2019). Today, GRACE is a $7 million organization and multi-service

[1] Churches involved in the initial start-up included First Baptist Church of Grapevine, First Methodist Church of Grapevine, Living Word Lutheran Church of Grapevine, Christ our King Church of Southlake, and St. Francis Catholic Church.

H. Hull Miori, *Millennial Philanthropy*,
https://doi.org/10.1007/978-3-031-30269-5_5

Fig. 5.1 Graceful Buys (Photo Credit: GRACE)

nonprofit which includes services spanning emergency assistance, a community health clinic, transitional housing, seasonal programs, resale stores, and donation centers (Fig. 5.1).

Many human service organizations receive as much as 40% of their budgets through government funding (Coletti 2018). However, GRACE does not receive any government funding and instead chooses to rely on fundraising from the community (GRACE 990 2019). For parachurch organizations like GRACE, religious channels provide a solid base for funding and volunteer support (Ammerman 2002; Baggett 2002). Special events include a signature gala, a golf tournament, a dine-around event, and a poker event. GRACE's philanthropic giving includes contributions (24%), special events (11%), grants (15%), donated goods and services (26%), donated use of facilities (1%), income from resale stores (22%), and other income (1%) (2020 GRACE Annual Report) (Fig. 5.2).

Roadmap for the Research

To analyze the results of the GRACE Philanthropy study, we will use the (by now familiar) social exchange theory, but we will also consider the effects of prosocial behavior theory when examining the role of millennials in philanthropy. Social exchange theory supports the interaction between different

Fig. 5.2 GRACE Gala: Auction Supports Fundraising (Photo Credit: GRACE)

groups including networks, social powers, and leadership groups (Cropanzano and Mitchell 2005, 874–75). The transaction includes an exchange of goods with rewards and costs (Nunkook and Haywantee 2012, 998). The gift-giving through a social exchange framework looks at the donor's self-interest and what the person gets in return, such as favorable recognition from peers (Mathur 1996, 107–8). In exchange for this increased esteem, the donor provides funding to the organization.

Prosocial behavior contends that "voluntary actions toward others can be learned and encouraged through external through external actions and situations" (Drezner 2009, 148). Prosocial behavior comes in different forms including (but not limited to) "comforting others, being cooperative, helping others and donating money, time or goods" (Kesberg and Keller 2021, 1). Philanthropy can reflect prosocial behavior through cash gifts and in-kind donations. Prosocial behavior theory explains altruism by focusing on one's self for the benefit of others, providing a framework for supporting the greater good.

To learn more about millennial philanthropy, four overarching questions guided the analysis of the data. The first asks whether *millennials have more philanthropic institutional loyalty (LTG score) than other generations.* Back in the 1990s, fundraising strategy began to move from one-time transactions tracking to donor lifetime value or lifetime giving (Drezner 2009, 150). In this study, this measurement is called LTG, which is designed to gauge the long-term value of a donor, which is important when thinking about the stability of the organization over time. The hypothesis is therefore asking whether even though millennials are younger, are donors giving more and staying longer with the organization, creating a higher LTG score that their generational counterparts.

The second question asks whether *millennials have more donor engagement (ENG) than other generations.* Engagement in this circumstance is total giving averaged by giving span for this study. Millennials seek engagement in new and multi-faceted ways and can deeply engage in a nonprofit due to their ability and desire to support the greater good and their community. As they come of age, the question asks how their capacity to engage compares to other generations.

The third question looks at whether *volunteering is associated with higher levels of donations.* Due to the lack of trust in institutions, research shows that millennial donations are tied to where they volunteer (Millennial Impact Report 2015). Volunteers are 58% more likely to support a charity financially after volunteering ("Time and Money: The Role of Volunteering in Philanthropy" 2021, 3). Per a post-pandemic cross-generational study by Fidelity Charitable, it was found that millennials decreased the number of organizations they volunteered at (slightly) compared to Baby Boomers and the Silent Generation; however, they are taking on more leadership roles and dramatically using specific skills to support the organizations they are involved in ("Time and Money: The Role of Volunteering in Philanthropy" 2021). Lifetime giving is also associated with volunteerism (James 2020), leading us to ask how millennial volunteering and philanthropy compares to other generations.

Finally, we want to investigate whether *gala attendance is associated with higher levels of donations.* Many nonprofits engage the community and donors through their galas. These high-end events often recruit gala chairs, volunteer committees, sponsors, celebrity speakers, entertainment, and high-end auctions. The dinners can provide an opportunity to "be seen," press for the organization, and an opportunity for the community to gather for the mission. Most of all, galas can support revenue and aim to promote more donations through and after the event (Kuhlman 2019). But do these events lead to millennial contributions, and if not what should come of them?

Data Collection and Analysis

Data from this study comes from the nonprofit organization Grapevine Relief and Community Exchange (GRACE). Data periods that were included were from 2014 to 2018. A quantitative analysis was completed from the GRACE database called Abila. The CRM software provides a unique opportunity because the organization tracks philanthropic support, volunteerism, and year of birth.

While maintaining anonymity, the organization provided unique numerical identifiers, constituent type (individuals, corporations, churches, foundations), and birthdays. The organization also gave gala attendance (2015–2018), volunteer hours (2015–2018), and a variety of information on individual donations. New variables were created and named including AvgGiving for average giving (total giving/gift count), LTVAVG for lifetime average (total giving/age), ENGVAL for donor engagement (total giving/giving span), and GivingSpan for the giving span or amount of time between the first and most recent gifts. I also created variables to signify which generation the potential donor belonged to (Silent Generation, Baby Boomer, Gen X, and Millennial). Individuals with no birth date or that were younger or older than these generations were removed from the analysis.

The study uses five different Ordinary Least Squares (OLS) and logistic regression analyses to understand the relationships between philanthropy, volunteering, philanthropic institutional loyalty, donor engagement, and event attendance (particularly for millennials).[2] Each of these factors can impact donor motivations and behavior.

Descriptive Statistics

The sample contains the following distribution of actual donors across generations. Prospects (or non-donors) were not used for the calculations (Table 5.1).

Lifetime average is total giving divided by age. This variable can provide an indicator for attachment to the organization for the lifetime of the donor by generation. Of the 3,376 observations, the mean for lifetime average is 9.86 with a standard deviation of 89.11. Average giving is total giving divided by gift count. The average is 255.44 with a standard deviation of 659.03. For the giving span, the average is less than a year at 0.84 but the standard deviation

---

[2] Please see Chapter 4 for an explanation of Ordinary Least Squares (OLS) Regression analysis.

Table 5.1 Donors by generation

Silent Generation	91	2.70%
Baby Boomers	813	24.08%
Gen X	1327	39.30%
Millennials	1145	33.92%
Total	3,376	100%

is 2.97. To continue to find how embedded or attached the donors are to GRACE, the average engagement value (total giving/giving span) is 742.69 with a standard deviation of 2,063.94 showing the variation.

Factors Influencing Philanthropy

Two variables were created called engagement (ENG) and lifetime giving (LTG) which show the funding support of the donors. The generation variables are Silent Generation, Baby Boomers, and Generation X with the reference group as millennials. Other variables analyzed include binary variables indicating volunteering during a certain year (volunteer 2014, volunteer 2015, volunteer 2016, volunteer 2017, and volunteer 2018) and gala attendance for a certain year (Gala 2015, Gala 2016, Gala 2017, and Gala 2018).

Factors Influencing Donation Amount for the Full Sample

I use the full sample to determine the relationship between generation and philanthropy using two different dependent variables: lifetime giving average (LTV) and giving span average (ENG) (Table 5.2).

As seen in Table 5.2, when looking at the factors influencing donations, lifetime giving has an *R*-square = 0.115, meaning the model explains 11.5% of the variance in the data. This means if the test is run over and over again, the variance would be low (a reliable test). In other words, lifetime giving plays a meaningful and significant role in donations. This is not a surprise for those who have been in fundraising for multiple years. Long-time donors who come back year and year are the lifeblood of organizations. And perhaps these persons are also engaging in other ways with volunteering, bringing other donors to the organization, and encouraging their family, friends, and colleagues to also become donors. Engagement has an *R*-square = 0.158,

Table 5.2 Factors influencing donation amount (full sample)

Variables	(1) LTG robust	(2) ENG robust
Silent Generation	−5.3906	−37.6670
	(4.122)	(27.020)
Baby Boomers	10.4123**	62.2089**
	(5.203)	(25.511)
Gen X	4.9961***	65.9937***
	(1.702)	(17.813)
Volunteer 2014	−0.0729	−0.9828
	(0.090)	(0.672)
Volunteer 2015	0.0084	1.4994
	(0.135)	(1.274)
Volunteer 2016	0.4302	1.7006
	(0.413)	(1.937)
Volunteer 2017	−0.1091	−0.1541
	(0.119)	(0.645)
Volunteer 2018	−0.0713	−0.5207
	(0.062)	(0.371)
Gala 2015	72.5865**	569.2547*
	(33.343)	(315.888)
Gala 2016	123.2412***	990.3431***
	(42.095)	(312.793)
Gala 2017	1.7331	−24.5854
	(8.813)	(66.757)
Gala 2018	42.6591	296.4385
	(31.306)	(232.731)
Constant	−0.6244	−3.2043
	(1.039)	(9.891)
Observations	3376	3376
R-squared	0.115	0.158
Prob > *F*	0.000	0.000

Standard errors in parentheses; ***$p < 0.01$, **$p < 0.05$, *$p < 0.1$

meaning the model explains 15.8% of variance in the data. The Prob > F indicates high significance, which means that the models are superior to intercept-only models.

When examining generations, Baby Boomers score higher for lifetime giving and engagement than millennials (the base group) at $p < 0.05$. This too is not surprising, as Baby Boomers have had a greater opportunity to gain wealth over a longer span of time to then give over more time than millennials. Recall that engagement is total giving divided by giving span. Engagement can be seen as prosocial behavior, and in the case of donating time, this theory lends itself to a more social services lens. At the same time, Generation X is statistically significant at $p < 0.1$ for Volunteer 2015 and Volunteer 2016, which impacts donation amount (and they are more impactful than Baby Boomers). In this instance, we see social exchange theory at work, providing the exchange of good feelings while the nonprofit gets the service of help and goods and services. In this dataset, Generation X is the better volunteers.

Compared to lifetime giving (LTG), neither Generation X nor Baby Boomers are volunteering at statistically significant levels more than millennials. When asking who are the best volunteers and how it impacts lifetime giving, there is no difference between our millennials, Generation X, and Baby Boomers. One puzzle is the 2015 Gala, which influenced donations at a significant level a $p < 0.1$ for engagement and lifetime giving at $p < 0.05$, though it is unclear what occurred during the event to cause this compared to other years.

When looking at donor loyalty and donor engagement (our first two questions), we see from the analysis that millennials do not have more philanthropic institutional loyalty (LTG score) than other generations nor more donor engagement (ENG) than other generations. But if they are like every other generation, is there anything that millennials are particularly good at?

Factors Influencing Donation Amount by Generation

To determine factors influencing donation amount at the generational level, I split the full sample into separate samples based on generation, then re-examined the relationship between generation and philanthropy using two different dependent variables: lifetime giving average (LTV) and giving span average (ENG). The regressions for Silent Generation and Millennials should be interpreted with caution based on the insignificant Prob > F. This means that we do not find evidence for or against our first two questions.

When thinking about if an analysis is a good fit, a test is run. For Baby Boomers' LTV (lifetime giving), the R-square = 0.011, meaning the model explains 1.1% of the variance in the data (which is very little). The Prob > F is at 0.178 and cautiously a good fit. For Baby Boomers' ENG (engagement), the R-square = 0.033, meaning the model explains 3.3% of the variance in the data (which is still low). The Prob > F is at 0.021 and cautiously provides a good fit, though the predictors do not explain much variance.

For Generation X lifetime giving, the R-square = 0.325, meaning the model explains 32.5% of the variance in the data. The R-squared is at 0.000 and a strong fit. Generation X shows engagement with an R-square = 0.287, meaning the model explains 28.7% of the variance in the data. The Prob > F is at 0.000 and a good fit. For Millennial LTV, R-square = 0.011, meaning the model explains 1.1% of the variance in the data (which is low). This makes sense based on their limited time to make gifts over a lifetime. The R-square is at 0.287 for X engagement and explains 28.7% of the variance reflects statistical significance at $p < 0.1$ for volunteering in 2015 and 2016. This offers very limited support for the claim that volunteering is associated with higher levels of donations (our third question). This is not surprising based on previous literature, but it is good to see a statistical affirmation of this as well (Table 5.3).

As seen in Table 5.3, when examining each generation, the role of volunteerism and the gala (questions three and four) could have impacted donations. For example, the Silent Generation is positively impacted by 2018 volunteerism and the 2015 Gala at the significant level $p < 0.1$ for lifetime giving and engagement level.

When examining each generation based on the result in Table 5.3, the role of gala attendance on donations is very limited but does have a positive response. Interestingly, millennials (whom we are interpreting with caution) share a statistically significant positive impact of 2016 gala attendance with Generation X. Gala attendance is a form of social exchange. The gala for the ticket holder has the opportunity to be "seen," receive a nice meal, opportunity to bid on auction items, network, and get dressed up. The nonprofit in exchange raises funds, utilizes their volunteers, and gets press. And in exchange both sides may have a good time—certainly in 2016 (Fig. 5.3).

Similarly, attendance at the 2015 Gala was significant for the Baby Boomers and the Silent Generation (whom we are interpreting with caution). What does this mean? While galas can be important and significant parts of our nonprofits works including staff time, volunteer resources, the divergence of funds, and the work of our nonprofits, galas (like any major events) need to be reviewed with the ultimate question in mind: "Are they worth a nonprofit's time?" The *Washington Post* calls galas a "contradictory event"—the organization is fundraising while spending arguably quite a bit of expense (Hackney and Middendorf 2017). Nonprofits must continue to balance the revenue, staff time, and expenses of these high-profile events and long-term impact of galas and high-profile events. In other words, while a gala can bring in the "big bucks," is it worth the time, effort, and sometimes heartburn and distraction and staff time away from other priorities? The data says for some generations only part of the time.

Table 5.3 Factors influencing donation amount, by generation

Variables	(1) Silent (LTV)	(2) Silent (ENG)	(3) BabyBoomer (LTV)	(4) BabyBoomer (ENG)	(5) X (LTV)	(6) X (ENG)	(7) Millennial (LTV)	(8) Millennial (ENG)
Volunteer 2014	−0.0000	−0.0138	0.0857	0.1798	−0.2252	−1.7431	−0.0038	−0.0312
	(0.008)	(0.139)	(0.103)	(0.322)	(0.221)	(1.934)	(0.005)	(0.071)
Volunteer 2015	0.0072	0.2980	−0.0683	−0.1175	0.1214	3.2013*	−0.0061	−0.0526
	(0.018)	(0.285)	(0.087)	(0.327)	(0.175)	(1.925)	(0.005)	(0.060)
Volunteer 2016	−0.0107	−0.4232	−0.0064	−0.1723	1.1471	5.7153*	−0.0068	−0.0351
	(0.019)	(0.330)	(0.029)	(0.163)	(0.737)	(3.237)	(0.011)	(0.153)
Volunteer 2017	0.0057	0.3178	−0.0525	−0.0563	−0.0406	0.3474	−0.0269	−0.5967
	(0.012)	(0.194)	(0.070)	(0.281)	(0.051)	(0.626)	(0.018)	(0.551)
Volunteer 2018	−0.0091***	−0.1306**	0.0842	0.4427	−0.0432	−0.1291	−0.0033	0.0506
	(0.003)	(0.058)	(0.123)	(0.430)	(0.037)	(0.270)	(0.007)	(0.176)
Gala 2015	7.2521***	324.0861***	77.4948*	717.0705*	68.8594	432.7394		
	(0.601)	(5.933)	(44.556)	(376.573)	(43.611)	(416.101)		
Gala 2016	–	–	38.6547	392.1880	107.3604**	957.9600***	22.0559***	787.7511***
			(46.077)	(265.166)	(42.466)	(339.884)	(0.437)	(7.342)
Gala 2017	–	–	90.2329	551.1439	45.9550	228.5933	33.9286	1240.6949
			(108.445)	(521.796)	(33.488)	(260.316)	(27.550)	(994.977)
Gala 2018	–	–			1.0390	−13.8173		
					(8.576)	(65.418)		
Constant	1.9638***	21.4876***	14.0198***	90.0216***	0.1343	31.1231*	1.1575*	14.0939*
	(0.594)	(5.958)	(5.062)	(23.216)	(2.485)	(17.812)	(0.654)	(7.294)
Observations	91	91	813	813	1327	1327	1145	1145
R-squared	0.029	0.338	0.011	0.033	0.325	0.287	0.011	0.093
Prob > *F*			0.178	0.021	0.000	0.000		

$^{***}p < 0.01$, $^{**}p < 0.05$, $^{*}p < 0.1$

Fig. 5.3 GRACE Gala: Auction Close-Up (Photo Credit: GRACE)

Factors Influencing Donation Decision (Full Sample)

To determine factors influencing donation decisions for the full sample, I divide the donation amount decision into two steps: the decision to donate and the amount to donate. With a larger and more complex dataset, this would involve a selection model such as a Heckman. However, since that is not possible with the current novel dataset, I instead model each decisions separately. We still learn a thing or two that can impact the way we look at our philanthropy.

In this section, I look at the decision to donate using OLS and logistic regression for the full sample, which allows us to compare generations. In the first step, the R-square $= 0.207$, meaning the model explains 20.7% of the variance in the data. The Prob > F is at 0.000 and is a good fit. The results once again show that millennials do not have more philanthropic institutional loyalty (LTG score) than other generations nor more donor engagement (ENG). Compared to millennials, all generations (Silent Generation, Baby Boomers, and Generation X) are statistically significant at $p < 0.01$. Baby Boomers will be better givers or supporters than millennials. At the same time, volunteering is almost entirely statistically insignificant based on the full sample, so there is no statistical support for the third question—whether volunteering is associated with higher levels of donations (though there is still an impact). Interestingly, gala attendance for Gala 2015, Gala 2016, and Gala 2018 is statistically significant at $p < 0.01$. The results provide support for gala attendance being associated with higher levels of donations. Though it is not every year, it shows up for three of the five years analyzed, which could indicate a possible trend that the gala can impact donations.

Table 5.4 Factors influencing donation decision full sample

Variables	(1) OLS	(2) Logit
Silent Generation	0.3019***	2.851***
	(0.051)	(0.287)
Baby Boomers	0.3257***	2.9121***
	(0.018)	(0.191)
Gen X	0.1475***	1.9481***
	(0.012)	(0.191)
Volunteer 2014	0.0003	0.0025
	(0.000)	(0.002)
Volunteer 2015	0.0001	−0.0004
	(0.000)	(0.002)
Volunteer 2016	−0.0002	−0.0014
	(0.000)	(0.002)
Volunteer 2017	−0.0002*	−0.0016
	(0.000)	(0.002)
Volunteer 2018	0.0003*	0.0022
	(0.000)	(0.002)
Gala 2015	0.3361***	3.1348***
	(0.057)	(0.668)
Gala 2016	0.5491***	
	(0.048)	
Gala 2017	−0.0265	−0.3400
	(0.030)	(0.264)
Gala 2018	0.3206***	3.3384***
	(0.066)	(0.719)
Constant	0.0284***	−3.5227***
	(0.005)	(0.175)
Observations	3376	3314
R-squared	0.207	
Prob > F	0.000	
Pseudo-Rsq		0.167
Prob > chi2		0.000

Robust standard errors in parentheses
*** $p < 0.01$, ** $p < 0.05$, * $p < 0.1$

Factors Influencing Donation Decision by Generation

When determining factors influencing donation decisions at the generational level, the Silent Generation and Millennials should be interpreted with caution, similar to the last generational regressions. This means we are unable to speak to LTG and ENG directly. We start by testing all generations against all volunteerism. The Baby Boomers have an R-square $= 0.035$, meaning the model explains 3.5% of the variance in the data. For Generation X, the R-square $= 0.201$, meaning the model explains 20.1% of the variance in the data. The R-squared is cautiously a good fit, particularly when compared to the other generations. Generation X is statistically significant at $p < 0.1$ for volunteerism in 2014, 2017, and 2018, supporting the notion that volunteering is associated with higher levels of donations (Table 5.5).

Table 5.5 Factors influencing donation decision by generation

	(1)	(2)	(3)	(4)
Variables	Silent	BabyBoom	X	Millennial
Volunteer 2014	−0.0004	0.0002	0.0011*	−0.0000
	(0.002)	(0.000)	(0.001)	(0.000)
Volunteer 2015	0.0012	−0.0005	0.0002	0.0002
	(0.002)	(0.001)	(0.000)	(0.000)
Volunteer 2016	−0.0020	−0.0001	0.0001	0.0001
	(0.002)	(0.000)	(0.000)	(0.000)
Volunteer 2017	0.0019	−0.0007	−0.0001*	−0.0001
	(0.002)	(0.001)	(0.000)	(0.000)
Volunteer 2018	−0.0017***	0.0015**	0.0003*	−0.0002
	(0.000)	(0.001)	(0.000)	(0.000)
Gala 2015	0.6353***	0.5191***	0.2643***	
	(0.062)	(0.084)	(0.075)	
Gala 2016		0.5114***	0.5347***	0.9688***
		(0.110)	(0.056)	(0.019)
Gala 2018		0.1515	0.3423***	0.6420**
		(0.209)	(0.070)	(0.269)
Gala 2017			−0.0234	
			(0.030)	
Constant	0.3635***	0.3562***	0.1720***	0.0264***
	(0.062)	(0.018)	(0.011)	(0.007)
Observations	91	813	1327	1145
R-squared	0.046	0.035	0.201	0.066
Prob > *F*		0.000	0.000	

Robust standard errors in parentheses
*** $p < 0.01$, ** $p < 0.05$, * $p < 0.1$

Factors Influencing Donation Amount (Only Donors)

In this section, we focus on the full sample (putting everything together), but only those who have already made the decision to donate (many CRMs include the names of prospective donors (non-donors) into their database). In other words, non-donors were not evaluated. Engagement matters more in this regression since the giving span matters more, though it is still not statistically significant except for the Silent Generation. Volunteerism impacts engagement at the $p < 0.05$ level for 2015 and 2016 years. Engagement is statistically significant for volunteerism for 2014 and volunteerism 2015 and Gala 2016 for $p < 0.05$. The lifetime giving is statistically significant at $p < 0.1$ for volunteerism for 2016 and 2017 and Gala 2016. Early volunteering matters for engagement since these activities take time over a giving span and the volunteer can have the opportunity for time to both volunteer and donate. Lifetime giving can impact recent volunteering. Weak support exists for volunteering and gala attendance being associated with higher levels of donations (Table 5.6).

The first question examines the philanthropic institutional loyalty (LTG) of millennials against other generations measured with lifetime giving. As a reminder, lifetime giving is total giving divided by age, so age factors into the equation and will influence the analysis. Based on this, lifetime giving had non-millennials (Silent Generation, Baby Boomers, and Generation X) giving more. This could be because other generations are older and have more years or opportunities of time to give and/or because older generations are known to have more wealth as an age cohort so they have the ability to give more. The best donors were in order were Silent Generation at $430.56 more than millennials in lifetime giving to the organization, followed by Baby Boomers at $168.64, and then Generation X (though at only $6.37 more than millennials). Although once again millennials are not shown to have more philanthropic institutional loyalty (LTG score) than other generations, there's reason for optimism. If you think about a lifetime, there is plenty of time for millennials to "catch up" on lifetime giving—especially given they are already on the heels of Generation X. For this particular case study, the millennial generation as a cohort is only giving $430 less over the time of the study than the Silent Generation and proportionally relative to other generations. As an organization and a fundraiser, I would, therefore, welcome this donor base—but how much time and attention do nonprofits give the millennial generation?

The created variable Engagement also shows an attachment score to the institution (i.e., the length of attachment to the organization). Per Table 5.6,

Table 5.6 Factors influencing donation amount, only donors

Variables	(1) LTV	(2) ENG
Silent Generation	−0.2998	−430.5641**
	(19.70)	(213.795)
Baby Boomers	12.0696	−168.6446
	(22.184)	(215.116)
Gen X	4.5845	−6.3657
	(19.625)	(220.067)
Volunteer 2014	−0.3332	−4.4273**
	(0.254)	(1.809)
Volunteer 2015	0.0852	3.9608**
	(0.233)	(1.883)
Volunteer 2016	1.4897*	5.5352
	(0.803)	(4.340)
Volunteer 2017	−0.8253*	−0.8055
	(0.491)	(4.201)
Volunteer 2018	−0.0941	−1.1345
	(0.073)	(0.978)
Gala 2015	65.1806*	459.7011
	(34.198)	(313.750)
Gala 2016	77.6699*	682.5859**
	(45.793)	(331.805)
Gala 2017	8.8795	−96.5019
	(35.137)	(265.758)
Gala 2018	57.9853	333.7936
	(35.745)	(259.534)
Constant	21.5474	375.0743*
	(18.081)	(206.393)
Observations	653	653
R-squared	0.150	0.171
Prob > F	0.001	0.000

Robust standard errors in parentheses
*** $p < 0.01$, ** $p < 0.05$, * $p < 0.1$

members of the Silent Generation are the better givers and their attachment is deeper than other generations. They are giving better than millennials over time, showing the significance of their role, their future giving, and their attachment score. These results do of course mean that they have more donor engagement than millennials, giving us our answer for question two (for those that have donated).

The third question is whether volunteerism increased donations. We found a surprising impact for Generation X—their giving was impacted by engagement, a donation decision, and lifetime giving (though this was a bit weak).

However, the results overall generally do not support the idea that volunteering is associated with higher levels of donations—or prosocial behavior as a motivator (more generally volunteering engages with prosocial behavior because the person is working with the greater good: they are not receiving anything in exchange such as food or "being seen").

For the question of whether gala attendance is associated with higher levels of donations, we know that attendance offers an opportunity to give time plus money, the opportunity to be seen at a high-profile event, an exchange of a meal for the price of admission, and even the ability to direct where funding goes (unlike a general fundraising appeal). This aligns well with social exchange theory. The person gets a ticket or sponsorship in exchange for a meal and entertainment for the gala attendance. The event also comes with a social scene and an opportunity to earmark his or her gift. The gala is also a high-profile event so they are going to attend for the opportunity in exchange for a social activity. The results support the idea that volunteering is associated with higher levels of donations, and social exchange theory explains why.

Implications

Millennials have the opportunity to impact our nonprofit communities in different ways and for different reasons than other generations. The GRACE Philanthropy study can help the nonprofit community pinpoint the best ways to engage the largest generation in the United States.

Aside from the insights on gala attendance and volunteering being predictors of giving, this study also offered us another insight when we split the sample into generations. The model was bad at predicting the giving behavior of the Silent Generation and Millennials when they were analyzed independently. For the Silent Generation, perhaps this was because advancing age keeps them from volunteering or attending the gala or galas aren't their scene; there could be physical reasons that this is an ill-fitting model. However, this is not the case for millennials. Though it did not set out to do this, this study also provides evidence that a model which is a very good fit for predicting Generation X giving is simultaneously a bad fit for predicting Millennial giving. So this study also provides quantitative empirical support for a conclusion from Chapter 2: nonprofits need to rethink engagement for millennials. If the "days of chicken and broccoli dinners are dead," how should they be engaged?

Though millennials still donate, the GRACE Philanthropy study reveals that Baby Boomers are better supporters than millennials. But this raises a deeper question: do the giving and philanthropy concerns lie with millennials or with how nonprofits are engaging the generation? The GRACE gala was only significant one year, so what happens in the wake of COVID-19 when nonprofits that have leaned on galas for years can't host them? More particularly, what can nonprofits do to gain the attention of a whole generation for funding? Nonprofits like GRACE should pay attention to millennial behavior—including donations and volunteerism—when trying to engage the largest generation.

Previous literature shared that millennials want to donate where they volunteer, but the GRACE data in Table 5.4 did not support this finding. Does GRACE need to find volunteer opportunities for millennials that will inspire funding? We know from generational theory and social exchange theory that millennials can give for longer than other generations and are influenced by certain events and activities. For example, some of the GRACE volunteer opportunities are on the front lines of the mission including the food pantry and medical clinic for the social services the organization offers. When millennials care about social justice and the opportunity to volunteer is hands on, we see "volunteering in action." An organization and fundraising community will need to ask themselves about their practices, options to give, and social justice and social service opportunities that link to philanthropy.

References

Ammerman, Nancy T. 2002. "Connecting Mainline Protestant Churches with Public Life." In *The Quiet Hand of God: Faith-Based Activism and the Public Role of Mainline Protestantism*, edited by R. Wuthnow and J. H. Evans. University of California Press.

Baggett, Jerome P. 2002. "The Irony of Parachurch Organizations: The Case of Habitat for Humanity." *New Directions for Philanthropic Fundraising* 2002, no. 35: 55–78.

Coletti, Joseph. 2018. "Strengthening Human Services With and Without Government." (January 8). Accessed December 30, 2022. https://www.johnlocke.org/strengthening-human-services-with-and-without-government/.

Cropanzano, Russell, and Marie S. Mitchell. 2005. "Social Exchange Theory: An Interdisciplinary Review." *Journal of Management* 31, no. 6: 874–900.

Drezner, Noah. 2009. "Why Give? Exploring Social Exchange and Organization Identification Theories in the Promotion of Philanthropic Behaviors of African-American Millennials at Private-HBCs." *International Journal of Educational Advancement* 9, no. 3: 147–65.

"GRACE Annual Report 2020." 2020. Accessed September 27, 2021. https://www.gracegrapevine.org/wp-content/uploads/2021/09/FY2020-Final-Annual-Report.pdf.

GRACE 990. 2018. Accessed September 27, 2021. https://www.gracegrapevine.org/wp-content/uploads/2021/08/2019-Public-Disclosure-Tax-form-990.pdf.

GRACE 990. 2019. Accessed September 27, 2021. https://www.gracegrapevine.org/wp-content/uploads/2021/08/GRACE-FY20-990.pdf.

GRACE Website. 2021. Accessed October 20, 2021. https://www.gracegrapevine.org/.

Hackney, Philip and Brian Mittendorf. 2017. "Charity Galas Can Waste Money. And the IRS Doesn't Always Notice When They Do." Accessed October 20, 2021. https://www.washingtonpost.com/news/posteverything/wp/2017/09/26/charity-galas-can-waste-money-and-the-idoesn'tsnt-always-notice-when-they-do/.

James, Russell. 2020. "Lifetime Giving, Volunteering Key To Estate Gifts." *The Nonprofit Times*, September 9, 2020.

Kesberg, Rebekka, and Johannes Keller. 2021. "Donating to the 'Right' Cause: Compatibility of Personal Values and Mission Statements of Philanthropic Organizations Fosters Prosocial Behavior." *Personality and Individual Differences* 168: 110313.

Kuhlman, Krista. 2019. "Eight Fundraising Gala Must-Haves." Accessed October 20, 2021. https://afpglobal.org/eight-fundraising-gala-must-haves.

Mathur, Anil. 1996. "Older Adults' Motivations for Gift Giving to Charitable Organizations: An Exchange Theory Perspective." *Psychology & Marketing* 13, no. 1: 107–23.

Millennial Impact Report. 2015. Accessed May 30, 2017. http://www.themillennialimpact.com/past-research.

Nunkook, Robin, and Haywantee Ramkissoon. 2012. "Power, Trust, Social Exchange and Community Support." *Annals of Tourism Research* 39, no. 2: 997–1023.

Sargeant, Adrian, and Jen Shang. 2010. *Fundraising Principles and Practice*. Jossey-Bass.

"Time and Money: The Role of Volunteering in Philanthropy." 2020. Accessed October 9, 2021. https://www.fidelitycharitable.org/content/dam/fc-public/docs/insights/volunteering-and-philanthropy.pdf.

6

Who's Next?: Paper for Water Generation Z Case Study

Whether it be for their financial health, workforce, or fundraising revenue, nonprofits need to strive for stability to look to the future of their respective organizations. By asking the question "What's next?," we naturally turn our eyes to the next generation. More than half of the nation's total population are now members of the millennial generation or younger (Frey 2020). That means persons born around 1980 or later are the largest segment of the US population. This surprising realization shows the need to turn our attention to the "youth" in the United States when we talk about the future of the nonprofit and fundraising scene. Previous chapters examined the nonprofit landscape through case studies from the perspective of the millennial generation, so it is logical that we should end by turning our attention to Generation Z (born between 2000 and 2011), which contains 70 million potential donors and volunteers (Seemiller and Grace 2019, 28).

Like with the millennial generation, we need to ask whether this generation is actually giving and volunteering, and if the answer is yes, what does the philanthropic landscape look like for Gen Z now and in the future? To get a better understanding of the philanthropy of this generation, we will look at the nonprofit Paper for Water (which legally files its IRS documents under Keiki International). When I was a younger fundraiser, I had the privilege of meeting Katherine and Isabelle Adams through their father. They were only 6 and 9 years old, but had already jumped into the philanthropic scene a year earlier. Through a lot of luck, the heart of some great young kids, and

H. Hull Miori, *Millennial Philanthropy*,
https://doi.org/10.1007/978-3-031-30269-5_6

some great volunteers, Paper for Water went from a novel idea into a full-scale philanthropic organization. Today, it attracts not just lots of Generation Z volunteers but national and international attention and many loyal board members (including myself). As of 2022, they have funded more than 200 water wells around the world and sanitation projects in over 20 countries by partnering with organizations to support the construction of wells and sanitation projects. We will navigate its history on how some scraps of paper have brought water to the thirsty all over the world.

As we look at the generational trends for Gen Z with respect to volunteerism and philanthropy, we will see that some are the same as the millennial generation (namely their technology connections), but also note how with this younger generation some trends—like values, social justice, and how they engage the world around them—are changing.

About Generation Z

Generation Z is sandwiched between the Millennial Generation (1980–1999) and Generation Alpha (2012–present). Like any generation, some members will be "cuspers" and this generation has been clumped by demographers into a smaller age range due to expedited technology changes and rapid shifts with respect to social media, smartphones, and the death of the landline. Commonly known as Gen Z, this generation has also been called the "i-generation" or "net-gen" and has never lived without digital devices (Turner 2015, 104; Serbanescu 2022, 62). This generation has therefore always grown up with social media, but also with an ever-present awareness of social justice and a desire for work-life balance. Generation Z therefore does have remnants of millennial trends affecting them, but they are forging their own path. Since its earliest members are now joining the workforce and entering colleges, this generation is also dipping its toes into the philanthropic scene as donors and in the workforce as members of nonprofit organizations.

The literature about Generation Z discusses workforce development, psychology, higher education, and consumer behavior (Turner 2015; Zietdinov and Cilliers 2021; Singh and Dangmei 2016). But first and foremost is their alignment with technology. As digital natives, Gen Z is navigating new roles in a "fast information society" (Serbanescu 2022, 62). When asked a question, Gen Zers no longer look something up in a book, but seek the information they need on a smartphone or a computer. As an entrepreneurial and tech-savvy generation, their attitude toward technology is different than previous generations (Hodges 2019, 3). Instead of waiting for technology to come to them, they are often creating the technology or making content. Members of Gen Z want to co-create culture rather than merely consume it (Hodges 2019, 3). The co-creation can come from social media or artificial intelligence, but like millennials they still are looking for authenticity. Genuine engagement will be a huge factor for nonprofits with this generation, as they must be careful not to look "manufactured" and embrace transparency. Due to the "instant society" Gen Z is growing up in, members will be quick to judge philanthropic efforts, but also willing to dive deep into topics if interested and be a tremendous advocate if asked. They may even spend hours online researching your mission.

It is not surprising this generation has a lack of healthy coping skills, including shorter attention spans—there's a reason TikTok is one of their favorite apps (Turner 2015, 107). Social media created connectivity but at the same time the concern of the fear of missing out (FOMO). Between technology and a global pandemic that forced everyone online, the information we have about their behavior is not surprising. These digital natives do it all: computers, social media, internet, and phones (Serbanescu 2022, 62). They are even called the "Philanthro-kids" by the industry due to their hyper-engagement and tech-savvy behavior within the philanthropic landscape (Berg 2022).

Gen Zers are also more likely to have a college-educated parent than previous generations (Schaeffer 2021); yet in contrast to their parent's generation, some interpret college degrees "as an obstacle to the American dream" (Gilchrist 2022, 49). Generation Z youth have been affected by the growing income gap and shrinking middle class (Turner 2015, 214).

As you might recall from earlier chapters, generations are marked by memories of key events. While each generation has memories of major world events and interactions with technology, *how* the generation remembers any wars, major events like weather events, tragedies, political changes, or technology changes the way it sees the world. In the case of Generation Z, it sees the world through young eyes. Generation Z does not have a recollection of September 11, 2001, and they were relatively young during the 2007–2008 recession. More pressing events are likely recent ones, like living through the COVID-19 pandemic or remembering and maybe participating in the Black Lives Matters movement. This information is similar to the millennial generation, but the young age this group had to reconcile these events primarily through technology, and that means they felt them differently.

For example, Generation Z was generous during the COVID-19 pandemic. One survey noted Generation Z came in as the second most generous generation after the millennials, often giving more than once (Leonhardt 2020). In this instance, we see patterns of giving coming early. Similar to millennials, authenticity and transparency are critical to gaining this generation's support; an organization's mission, values and effectiveness must be consistent in brand messaging and donor communications (Changing our World and One World, 4, n.d.). 70% percent of Gen Zers shared in a survey that they are " loyal, thoughtful, determined, compassionate, open-minded, and responsible" (Seemiller and Grace 2019, 29). This information complements the desire of this generation to want to have authentic messaging from brands including nonprofits.

Generation Z displays complex and oftentimes seemingly contradictory behaviors (Luttrell and MacGrath 2021, 49). They will often be loners sitting among themselves engrossed in their technology (Gilchrist 2022, 44) as this style of media creates a distraction for many of the young persons. Media Company *We Are Social* noted that the average attention span for ad campaigns for a member of Gen Z is only 8 seconds (Young 2018). However, they still like to do things *IRL* ("in real life"). For example, 61% prefer to shop in stores, and 80% were planning to shop in-person during the holiday season (Cullen 2019). The role of millennials and Generation Z continues to be filled with social media consumption, but each is different. Unlike millennials, who crave experiences and the next social media picture, Generation Z prefers cool products over cool experiences (Hodges 2019, 3).

Racial Diversity and Social Justice

In the literature, we find that this generation is more racially diverse than any preceding it, with one in four being Hispanic. As a result, the social landscape has changed from previous generations (Schaeffer 2021). This generation also includes "new minorities," a term coined by Frey for those who identify as Asian or dual-race (Frey 2011, 22). As a result, 49% of the generation identifies as nonwhite (Seemiller and Grace 2019, 30). These racial profiles weave a landscape that will drive the work of philanthropies in how they fundraise and communicate their messaging. Already, 23% of the US House of Representatives and Senate are members of a racial or ethnic minority. A study by Pew Research Center illustrates the trend toward a more diverse representation (Schaeffer 2021). Ethnicity and race are important identity markers that reflect greater diversity (Katz et al. 2021, 42). It begs the question of how other aspects of representation will surface in the form of communication, leadership, and other areas of philanthropy (Schaeffer 2021).

Generation Z has had a disruptive upbringing due to culture and politics (Gilchrist 2022, 47). They are living in a time where social justice movements have called youth to the frontlines as vocal activists and key players in shaping the future (Powell et al. 2021, 56). Gen Z often uses social media as a megaphone for their activism. This generation also has a "self-imposed obligation to fight perceived injustices and right the wrongs within their society" (Luttrell and MacGrath 2021, 50). As a result, this generation wants not just to see diversity represented, but advocates for racial justice, equity, and inclusion from the brands it supports. Their desire to impact racial justice comes through on social media to make a difference (Powell et al. 2021, 56). Their goal is not just to see statements against racial injustice, but to see action. In particular, 70% of Generation Z supports companies that genuinely engage in social justice (PN Purpose Tracker 2020).

Digital Natives

The fact that this generation is also called iGen communicates a message about how they engage with social media. Unlike the previous generation of millennials who remember the advent of home computers and Steve Jobs unveiling the iPhone in his black turtleneck, Generation Z has always experienced computers at home and school, along with smartphones and high-speed internet. For Gen Z, brand loyalty is evident in social media—in particular their affinity for Snapchat (Weise 2015). However, the role of social media quickly evolves, and Gen Z is quick to adopt the new "it" app, be it Parler, Be Real, or other channels for work, play, or networking. These "mobile prodigies" use social media channels in all aspects of life, and for them technology in the form of the "internet, email, social media, platforms, and virtual meetings" plays a critical role (Serbanescu 2022, 61; Luttrell and MacGrath 2021, 47). Their consumption of social media is not limited to the likes of Facebook, Snapchat, Instagram, and LinkedIn, and nonprofits must recognize the full array of platforms they use and how younger generations are interacting with each other.

Interestingly, Gen Z wants their brands to be authentic and creative, yet nevertheless use an influencer (Weise 2015). This ideology tells nonprofits that they have to be careful how they push out their messaging to this "technology-obsessed" generation, which is both "cautious" and "individualistic" and always trying to stand on their own (Schnapp et al. 2022). While during interviews millennials speak to the era of pre- and post-social media and different channels becoming popular (Miori 2020), Generation Z will only remember the days of social media in the home, school, and in the workforce. As a result of these technology changes, this generation has a shorter timeframe focus (Katz et al. 2021, 42).

How Gen Z Differs from Millennials

One way to think about the differences is in how each generation is labeled. Generation Z is called the "We" generation, while millennials are called the "Me" generation (Seemiller and Grace 2019, 275). Generation Z will also be known as "the great disruptor"—the old systems and status quo will be disrupted as a result of their actions (Seemiller and Grace 2019, 275).

Interestingly, unlike our millennial generation where parental influence is not robust, this generation has their lives posted on social media by their parents and grandparents (Seemiller and Grace 2019, 105). 89% of those in Generation Z rank their parents as the biggest influence on their values (Seemiller and Grace 2019, 105). This is a dramatic shift from millennials, despite the fact that their parents are generally coming from the millennial generation or Generation X.

When we look at the workforce perspective of this generation, we can begin to gain another perspective of how they differ from previous generations. Generation Z has responded differently to other world events and is more pragmatic, prefers job security, and is risk averse ("Understanding Generation Z in the Workplace" n.d.; Luttrell and MacGrath 2021, 51). These personality traits also impact their perspective on having an entrepreneurialism spirit (or lack thereof). Some studies show that Generation Z will make up 27% of the workforce by 2025 (Staglin 2022). In the wake of COVID-19 and technological advances, they want flexibility, and many companies are providing remote work or at least hybrid schedules.

These personality traits flow into other parts of their lives as well. Gen Z will be a collaborator, "show self-confidence," want to see their path for the future, and put a scale on their "happiness at the workplace" (Goh and Lee 2018, 21). In sum, a typical Gen Zer is a self-driver who deeply cares about others, strives for a diverse community, is highly collaborative and social, and values flexibility, relevance, authenticity, and non-hierarchical leadership. While dismayed about inherited issues like climate change, Generation Z has a pragmatic attitude about the work that has to be done to address these issues (Witte 2022). These factors will begin to influence how they look at the nonprofit sector.

About Paper for Water

What would you do if you learned a child dies every 15 seconds because they do not have access to water? Enter 8-year-old Isabelle and 5-year-old Katherine back in 2012. They learned from a community member about the need for water in other countries and the beginnings of Paper for Water began. These Generation Zers started to get involved by making origami to sell to raise funds to help this global crisis, and soon roped in their friends and family, their congregation, and everyone else they knew to help them cut, fold, and create beautiful creations (Fig. 6.1).

Fig. 6.1 Photo Credit: Paper for Water

Per their website, the group uses origami to achieve some ambitious aims.

While we effect change abroad, we are also working to create a local movement in our North Texas community. To be more precise, Paper for Water:

- Provides access to clean water and sanitation for the global poor worldwide;
- Educates others about the world water crisis;
- Promotes servant leaders who follow Christ's message to serve with joy and compassion;
- Uses the creativity and energy of our local community to connect individuals and transform the world;
- Emphasizes character building through living a meaningful and purposeful life;
- Equips and develops leaders; and
- Empowers an entrepreneurial spirit that seeks solutions for the world's problems (Paper For Water Website 2022; Paper For Water YouTube Channel 2022).

What began as a small $500 donation from the girls' first origami show at a local Starbucks has grown considerably. Things went into hyperspeed after a meeting some local executives. Nine months after starting, the girls flew to New York to speak at a United Nations Women's meeting. Things progressed into a registered 501c3 and a goal of $50,000 for ten water wells. The Association of Fundraising Professionals (AFP) Dallas Chapter recognized them with the Youth in Philanthropy award, a local faith-based organization honored them, and then a national mainpage Yahoo article about them received wide circulation.

Within a year of starting their group, the girls met both celebrities and large philanthropists. It came from thinking big, some luck, some faith, and keeping doors open. The "pieces" kept coming together and then their big break happened—a documentary (*The Halo Effect*) featured the girls and their fellow Gen Z volunteers coming together to fold paper, ask others for money, and give their own precious few dollars to help (Fig. 6.2).

Paper for Water is now turning its focus from the international need for clean drinking water and looking within the United States. Partnering with Kleenex, there was an opportunity to film a family in the Navajo nation that needed water and partner with Dig Deep to dig their well. The opportunities continued with partnerships with Nickelodeon and then corporations like Lemi Shine and Neiman Marcus got involved and made the origami part of their Christmas catalog and their "fantasy gift" (Fig. 6.3).

Fig. 6.2 AFP Dallas and Youth in Philanthropy Award presentation with Adams family, Holly Hull Miori, and Scott Murray in 2012 (Photo Credit: Samuel Watters)

The organization has won corporate awards, gone to festivals, talked in places of worship, met elected officials and built out an impressive board. At this point, the group members are all in their early teens and the organization has raised millions. Their reach is getting bigger outside of Dallas, TX, and now the groups demographic is changing beyond just private schools to connect with public schools, church groups, and more. The Generation Z ripple effect is real. Due to age, parental influence typically gets kids initially connected through the various organizations the girls spoke at (many in this group were not allowed on the internet or social media).

Then the tides started to turn at the board meetings because Isabelle and Katherine started to take part and lead. In their book *One Piece of Paper at a Time*, Katherine recollects a full-scale presentation she was at by a Baby Boomer. She laughs at how the presenter used the typefont Curlz MT and the unicorns and rainbows they used. Generation Z is "mature youth" and does not want to be talked down to (Adams and Adams 2022, 171). The girls had the privilege and admittedly big opportunity to travel around the world. Their topic provided the chance to think big but engage locally. They were able work with Dig Deep and Living Water International and hear stories of

Fig. 6.3 Isabelle Adams and Katherine Adams with their Neiman Marcus fantasy tree (Photo Credit: Deb Adams)

how their gifts made an impact. Like many other philanthropic organizations, despite the COVID-19 pandemic this group pivoted and continued to teach volunteers how to fold origami, sell origami, and continued to raise funds for water wells and sanitation projects. During this time, Paper for Water was even gifted a professional space through a millennial board member, where the group celebrated its 10th anniversary. Also during this time, a youth council was created which was called Changemaker's Council. This group enabled members to be organized more formally, socialize, and be recognized for volunteer hours.

Roadmap for the Research

To learn more about the philanthropic work of Generation Z and Paper for Water, two overarching questions will be used for analysis:

- *How is Generation Z different from millennials?*
- *How is Generation Z similar to the millennials?*

Both generations are influenced by generational and societal factors and experience pressures stemming from politics, religion, environment, and economic factors. All of these areas come together and can impact the philanthropic landscape for various generations, including Generation Z and their millennial elders. But each generation reacts to these influences differently based on age and other experiences that their cohort had. Generation Z can be further influenced by their understanding of race, gender, the area of the country, or world they are from, family dynamics, and individual preferences. While this research discusses generalizations, it also recognizes that like a Rubik's cube, each generation is complex due to the uniqueness of the individuals that comprise it.

To explore these complexities, two theories were used to look deeper into Generation Z. Grounded theory offers a general method and framework which works from the "ground up" to generate a framework to help answer research questions, while generational theory sees persons uniting into generational cohorts who share common outlooks as a result of the framing experiences of major events while growing up. Both of these theories help us navigate the role of youth in philanthropy and answer our research questions of how both generation Z and millennials are alike and different in how they engage and react to the same societal influences.

Grounded Theory

The Grounded Theory Method was founded or "discovered" in the 1960s by Glaser and Strauss (Bryant and Charmaz 2007, 2). As its name suggests, the concept driving the theory is to work from the "ground up," starting with data and noting patterns that lead to more generalized theoretical constructs that can then be used to help answer research questions (Gibson and Hartman 2014, 2). The findings that use the theory can guide researchers to help provide structure to our insights stemming from the data and allows us to work from our findings to generalize such that the "theory emerges from the data" (Bryant and Charmaz 2007, 2). Grounded theory holds that so long as the researcher is nimble in the questions they ask and the people they ask them of, the answers they get will eventually allow them to extrapolate from what they learned and create a "form of knowledge production" (Gibson and Hartman 2014, 2).

Generational Theory

This theory was originally formulated by Mannheim in 1952 with the main pillars focused on location, actuality, and generational units (Pendergast 2009, 506). He observed that generations are "multidimensional social groups" within history (Shankar 2019, 106). The idea was extended further by Strauss and Howe when they argued that people in generations represent an "age group" that "share a distinct set of beliefs, attitudes, values, and behaviors" (Shankar 2019, 106; Gilchrist 2022, 47). Strauss and Howe maintain that a "generational constellation" appears every twenty to twenty-five years (Strauss and Howe 1991, 24).

Interview: Isabelle Adams

Biography

Isabelle Adams is 19 years old and a Generation Z and freshman in college. As one of the co-founders of Paper for Water, she raises money to fund water projects around the world. She has two younger sisters. Despite a large age difference, she notes they are really close. They were raised Presbyterian and have been very active in their church and sings in the choir. Eleven years ago, her younger sister and her started a nonprofit. Photo Credit: Roxanne Minnish

What is Your First Memory of Philanthropy?

My first memory of philanthropy is also one of my earliest memories. When I was really little, my mom would take me and my sister to a nursing home near our house and we would organize little parties for the residents. We went almost every month, and I distinctly remember how wonderful it was to help bring a smile to everyone's faces.

What is Your Family's Influence on Philanthropy?

My parents have been extremely influential in how I view philanthropy. Giving back has always been a way of life for them, and they have instilled this idea in me as well. There was never a question of if we would volunteer, but rather which project we would choose to help with.

What is the Last Gift You Made and Why?

The last gift I made would be my time. I sing in church every Sunday and the time and effort I give to the congregation are a big part of how I participate in my church.

What Has Been Your Personal Favorite Gift?

My favorite gift is the work that I have put into Paper for Water. It has been a labor of love with countless long days and overwhelming projects, but it has been incredibly rewarding.

How Did You Get Involved with the Nonprofits You Are Involved in?

Friends, family, and my church.

How Many Nonprofits Are You Engaged in?

I am actively involved with at least four nonprofits, and over the course of my life I have worked with many more.

How Did You Get Involved?

The main nonprofit I work with is the one that my sister and I started (Paper for Water), but I got involved with the other organizations through my church and my school mostly.

Do You Raise Funds for These Nonprofits, Give Personally, or Both?

I fundraise a lot for Paper for Water and I donate my time and expertise, but I rarely give monetary donations. I don't have a lot of disposable income, so the only place I donate to on a regular basis would be my church.

What is Your Generation's Biggest Influence in Philanthropy?

On the whole, I think my generation's biggest influence is our parents. The examples they and other authority figures in our lives set for us have a huge impact on the way we live our lives. If you grow up in a household where the expectation is to give back and you regularly volunteer with your family, the chances are that these practices will continue for the rest of your life.

What Do You Hope for Your Generation?

I hope that people will see that philanthropy not only benefits the receiver but also the giver.

In a world where it seems like people are constantly struggling to find meaning in their lives, helping other people never fails to make me feel like I am doing something important with my time and effort. I know the problems our world is facing often seem overwhelming, but if you can make even one person's day a bit better, you are helping to make the world a better place.

Data Collection

Information about the organization came from years of working knowledge with Paper for Water as a board member, secondary analysis on 990s, and utilizing publicly available information including social media channels, public events, and newsletters (Paper For Water Website 2022) (Fig. 6.4).

Factors Influencing Gen Z Philanthropy

If you think about Paper for Water in the context of this generation, no one was driving, no one was on social media yet, and the work was being motivated by their peers and parents. Indeed, per their biography *One Piece of Paper at a Time* (Adams and Adams, 1), they note their biggest influence for thinking big, being motivated and understanding philanthropy is their parents, which can be seen at events, the large-scale videos including the Kleenex commercial, *Halo Effect* documentary with Nickelodeon and even board meetings. Many of the Generation Z volunteers and changemakers learned of the organization from their parents (Paper For Water Website 2022; Paper for Water Board Meetings, 2017–2022; Paper for Water Youth Reports 2019, 2020; Paper for Water Ten Year Highlights 2021). However, despite their parents being the initial inspiration, we see the spirit of "sticking-to-it" has emerged within the generation. The documentary and annual reports tell a story of work from not only the Adams girls' perspective, illustrating that they are not just outliers for this generation. In fact, this group of Gen Zers had a ripple effect not only in the Dallas-Fort Worth area but across the United States, creating a "Halo Effect" (as the Nickelodeon documentary suggests).

When exploring the generation from the "ground up," we look at what impacts the work of this generation and what is similar and different from the preceding generation. Not surprisingly, this generation wants authenticity and to put their hands on their philanthropy. We see that in action with Paper for Water Generation Z volunteers. Their volunteerism comes with a desire to "get their hands dirty" and wanting to know where their work and funding goes. Paper for Water is accordingly clear about the projects it funds (Paper for Water 2021 Annual Report 2022; Paper For Water Website 2022). As seen in the group's communications (e.g., emails and annual reports), volunteers and donors can see their work in action and know what their hours of folding and dollars are going to—namely "bringing water one piece of paper at a time" (Paper for Water 2021 Annual Report 2022).

Fig. 6.4 Origami Installation at regional mall (Photo Credit: Deb Adams)

This is precisely where the two theories come together. Generational theory speaks to the "times we live in" and serves as one of the biggest influences for a young generation still "coming of age" (and despite uncertainties with the economy, a global pandemic and political unrest). As more digitally native than the preceding generation, they have a bit of distrust and will actually do even more face-to-face than expected but still maintain a digital and even global presence. Like their counterparts, they care about global crises, but want to make a local impact and have a hands-on opportunity to be part of the solution. They will also volunteer where they give, and bring their friends, family, and parents with them. Where Generation Z differs is their parents are a big influence on their values, and that also influences their philanthropy. It is unclear at this time if this will "stick" as they get older, so this will be an interesting question to investigate in the future.

Like any nonprofit, some volunteers are episodic or more sporadic. However, many volunteers of all ages are consistent and long-time volunteers (Paper for Water 2021 Annual Report 2022), and it turns out that many of them come from Generation Z. Per the 2021 Annual Report, six of the changemakers (all Generation Z) received the Presidential Volunteer Service Award (Paper for Water 2021 Annual Report 2022), and one even started a club at Southern Methodist University. Those volunteers that stay involved come at the issue from the lens of social justice, the opportunity to make a real impact and the ability to keep an eye on their volunteerism more than through a digital screen. Like the previous generation, the group wants to volunteer where they give, and although the generation's giving is small (and tracked very little), they will help get their parents, friends and help on social media (when allowed).

From a "ground up" perspective we can also investigate how these two generations are similar. Donor impact has been important as is the need for transparency. The origami put a spotlight on global issues in a way to make a local impact. The hands-on approach is also real and relevant to the research at hand. While we recognize this generation is not expected to give as much as older generations, and not much data is available compared to those generations, we expect them according to generational theory to continue to give as funds become more available (Fig. 6.5).

So what should nonprofits and the academic community do to prepare for youth volunteerism and philanthropy? Most importantly, they need to prepare the volunteer and philanthropic landscape through their messaging. This generation appreciates hands-on experience and wants to dive deep into the mission of an organization. Even when the issue is a global crisis, finding ways to make an issue local would be a great way to provide opportunities to engage them (and those they are connected to) in nonprofit organizations.

The other interesting finding from working with this nonprofit is the influence of their parents. What little is known in the literature focuses on how parents impact the values for this generation. But in this instance some of the parents also get involved, with the kids driving the decisions in coming

Fig. 6.5 Adams family on an international trip (Photo Credit: Samuel Watters)

to the table and debating how to get more people involved. However, their attention span is shorter, so it is up to nonprofits to successfully engage a whole generation and prepare for 70 million members of Generation Z as they continue to come of age.

References

Adams, Katherine, and Isabelle Adams. 2022. *One Piece of Paper at a Time* (Ten Year Anniversary Edition). Carpenter's Son Publishing.

Berg, Alice. 2022. Gen Z: The Generation of Donors. Accessed November 12, 2022. https://www.classy.org/blog/gen-z-next-generation-donors/.

Bryant, Antony, and Kathy Charmaz. 2007. *The SAGE Handbook of Grounded Theory*. Sage.

Cullen, Catherine. 2019. "4 things to know about Gen Z's holiday shopping habits." November 20. Accessed December 10, 2022. https://nrf.com/blog/4-things-know-about-gen-zs-holiday-shopping-habits.

Frey, William H. 2011. "America's Diverse Future: Initial Glimpses at the US Child Population from the 2010 Census." April. Accessed November 1, 2022. https://www.brookings.edu/wp-content/uploads/2016/06/0406_census_diversity_frey.pdf.

Frey, William. 2020. "Now More than Half of Americans Millennials or Younger." July 30. Accessed November 24, 2022. https://www.brookings.edu/blog/the-avenue/2020/07/30/now-more-than-half-of-americans-are-millennials-or-younger/.
Gibson, Berry, and Jan Hartman. 2014. *Rediscovering Grounded Theory*. Sage.
Gilchrist, Brian. 2022. "Everything Is An App (Including Us): The Media Ecology of Generation Z". In *Social Media, Technology, and New Generations: Digital Millennial Generation and Generation Z*, edited by Ahmet Atay and Mary Z. Ashlock. Lexington Books/Fortress Academic.
Goh, William, and Cindy Lee. 2018. "A Workforce to be Reckoned with: The Emerging Pivotal Generation Z Hospitality Workforce." *International Journal of Hospitality Management* 73: 20–28. https://doi.org/10.1016/j.ijhm.2018.01.016.
Goh, William H. 2014. *Diversity Explosion: How New Racial Demographics are Remaking America*. Brookings Institution Press.
Hodges, Dawn Z. 2019. "Use Generational Theory as a Guide to Understanding College Students." *Dean and Provost* 21 (3): 3.
Katz, Roberta R., Sarah Ogilvie, Jane Shaw, and Linda Woodhead. 2021. *Gen Z, Explained: The Art of Living in a Digital Age*. The University of Chicago Press.
Leonardt, Megan. September 30, 2020. Accessed November 1, 2022. https://www.cnbc.com/2020/09/29/more-millennials-donated-money-during-the-pandemic-than-other-generations.html.
Luttrell, Regina, and Karen McGrath. 2021. *Gen Z: The Superhero Generation*. Rowman & Littlefield Publishers.
Miori, Holly. 2020. "Millennial Philanthropy." Association of Fundraising Professionals Shreveport Monthly Meeting.
Pendergast, Donna. 2009. "Generational Theory and Home Economics: Future Proofing the Profession." *Family and Consumer Sciences Research Journal* 37 (4): 504–522.
Paper for Water Board Meetings. 2017–2022. *Meeting Minute Records*.
Paper For Water Website. 2022. Retrieved November 25, 2022. https://www.paperforwater.org.
Paper For Water Youtube Channel. 2022. Accessed December 1, 2022. https://www.youtube.com/@PaperForWater.
Paper for Water 2021 Annual Report. 2022. Accessed November 19, 2022. https://paperforwater.org/pdf/annual-report-2021.pdf.
Paper for Water Youth Report. 2019. Accessed December 1, 2022. https://paperforwater.org/youth-report.
Paper for Water Youth Report. 2020. Accessed December 1, 2022. https://paperforwater.org/pdf/PFW_Youth_Report2020.pdf.
Paper for Water Ten Year Highlights. 2021. Accessed December 15, 2022. https://paperforwater.org/landing-pages/timeline.
PN Purpose Tracker: Gen Z Joins the Social Justice Movement Wave IX. August 2020. Accessed December 4, 2022. https://www.porternovelli.com/wp-content/uploads/2021/01/03_Porter-Novelli-Purpose-Tracker-Wave-IX-Gen-Z-Joins-the-Social-Justice-Movement.pdf.

Schaeffer, Katherine. January 28, 2021. “Racial, ethnic diversity increases yet again with the 117th Congress.” Accessed December 6, 2021. https://www.pewresearch.org/fact-tank/2021/01/28/racial-ethnic-diversity-increases-yet-again-with-the-117th-congress/.

Schnapp, B. H., T. Cloyd, N. D. Hartman, T. Moadel, S. A. Santen, and M. Gottlieb. 2022. “Avocado Toasted: Mythbusting Millennials, Generation Z, and Generational Theory.” *AEM Education and Training* 6 (3): e10757. https://doi.org/10.1002/aet2.10757.

Seemiller, Corey, and Meghan Grace. 2019. *Generation Z Goes to College*. John Wiley & Sons.

Serbanescu, Anca. 2022. “Millennials and the Gen Z in the Era of Social Media.” In *Social Media, Technology, and New Generations: Digital Millennial Generation and Generation Z*, edited by Ahmet Atay and Mary Z. Ashlock. Lexington Books/Fortress.

Shankar, Shalini. 2019. *Beeline: What Spelling Bees Reveal About Generation Z's New Path to Success*. Basic Books.

Singh, Amarendra P., and Jianguanglung Dangmei. 2016. “Understanding Generation Z: The Future Workforce.” *South-Asian Journal of Multidisciplinary Studies* 3 (3): 1–5.

Staglin, Garen. July 22, 2022. “The Future Of Work Depends On Supporting Gen Z.” Accessed July 7, 2022. https://www.forbes.com/sites/onemind/2022/07/22/the-future-of-work-work-depends-on-supporting-gen-z/?sh=7eea26f5447a.

Powell, Aisha, Kapriatta Jenkins, Britney Gulledge, and Wei Sun. 2021. “Teaching Social Justice and Engaging Gen Z Students in Digital Classrooms during COVID-19.” *The Journal of Scholarship of Teaching and Learning* 21 (4). https://doi.org/10.14434/josotl.v21i4.32708

Strauss, William, and Neil Howe. 1991. “The Cycle of Generations.” *American Demographics* 13 (4): 9–33.

Turner, Anthony. 2015. “Generation Z: Technology and Social Interest.” *The Journal of Individual Psychology* 71 (2): 103–113.

Understanding Generation Z in the Workplace. n.d. Accessed December 7, 2022. https://www2.deloitte.com/us/en/pages/consumer-business/articles/understanding-generation-z-in-the-workplace.html.

Young, Katie. March 28, 2018. “Three Differences in How Gen Z and Millennials Use Social Media.” Retrieved on November 26, 2022. https://wearesocial.com/us/blog/2018/03/three-differences-gen-z-millennials-use-social-media/

Weise, Stephanie. December 11, 2015. “What We Learned from Gen Z 101.” Accessed November 26, 2022. https://wearesocial.com/us/blog/2015/12/learned-gen-101/.

Witte, Melissa de. 2022. Accessed November 21, 2022. https://news.stanford.edu/2022/01/03/know-gen-z/.

Ziatdinov, R., and J. Cilliers. 2021. “Generation Alpha: Understanding the Next Cohort of University Students.” *European Journal of Contemporary Education* 10 (3): 783–789.

7

Conclusion: How to Reach Millennial Donors

Millennials are complex—their intersectionality is like a Rubik's cube. While millennials have complex motivations, this generation's ability to make contributions to the nonprofit community can be unique and meaningful. The main findings of the studies we've looked at align with the literature. However, it is surprising to learn how much friends and peers influence millennials, showing the key role they play when it comes to fundraising and volunteering with nonprofits. This impact should be noticed by the fundraising and nonprofit community. How will they engage millennials while asking them to engage their social networks?

The desire of millennials to participate in fundraising events is no longer about high-ticket events, high-profile speakers, and society coverage. They will attend your events, but the viewpoint will come from a social justice lens. They will want to attend "genuine" but fun events that are still shareable on social media. When you ask them to come, how will you make a difference? Are you asking them to have a seat at the table and have a voice? The goal is about engagement and being connected to where they volunteer—because for the nonprofits they volunteer at, millennials also donate. As we shift to Generation Z, like their preceding generation they also appreciate a genuine viewpoint and events. While not as many are on social media, they do participate in content and watch and consume your fundraising events online. Look at the esports phenomenon! What can the nonprofit community learn from this?

H. Hull Miori, *Millennial Philanthropy*,
https://doi.org/10.1007/978-3-031-30269-5_7

Social media is an integral part of nonprofits to fundraise, engage, and inform all generations but in particular millennials. Organizations need to address shifts in the platforms that millennials use. These changes can often distract a nonprofit and use up time and energy while keeping them behind. A social media plan is necessary for nonprofits to reach the millennial generation, and this is especially important as the Great Transfer of Wealth looms. How will nonprofits respond? They need to get prepared with fundraising plans suitable for millennials. What digital microphone will you give them? And will you give them opportunities to engage their friends? When looking at your communications (which come from many different perspectives) can millennials and Generation Z see themselves? In particular for Generation Z, their social media content is more intense than their preceding generations. As a result of the global pandemic, this generation uses the internet to test boundaries, work through the world around them and find their way through the social justice lens.

While the information presented in this book offers broad-stroke opportunities for how to reach millennials, it also speaks optimistically to how we can reach out to this generation as donors, volunteers, and board members. The findings in this book have several implications. For example, friends and their generational peers play a crucial factor for millennials as they bring them to nonprofit organizations and influence their philanthropic giving. A nonprofit should look toward the donors' friends' circle, but the nonprofit industry must decide how they will utilize influential friends. The use of technology will be important, and forward-thinking organizations have found an expanded network via social media with millennials (Fig. 7.1).

While millennials care about members of their family and their well-being, they do not seem to be influenced by these family members on how to live their lives (and philanthropy). This generation wants to live their lives independently of their parents and elders. The nonprofit sector must shift to interacting directly with millennials rather than their parents.

Current theories are lacking on how to manage this generation—especially when it comes to volunteerism and philanthropy. During the GRACE study, we learn they do volunteer and lean to more social justice activities: feeding the hungry, translating for clients, and work in the medical clinic. For our nonprofit communities, no matter what the organization is, they need to begin examining their value and translating their amazing mission and vision for the lens of a millennial and Generation Z generations. From their volunteer hours and their philanthropic dollars and maybe even through their work, they can pull it all together and help nonprofits translate being

Fig. 7.1 BvB Game Day 2021 (Photo Credit: Mat Nelson)

part of the "greater good." However, your global issue may end up needing a local impact or something tangible for them to participate in.

For example, many millennials have lost their religion yet feel more spiritual. Since we have lost the traditional indicators for philanthropy, the nonprofit and academic community needs to continue to look for additional indicators regarding likeliness for giving. The book reveals that millennials feel the need to be engaged in social justice and technology. What do we do as a sector? Their experiences growing up also led to different outcomes: When everyone got a trophy, a whole generation absorbed an entrepreneurial spirit.

We know from interviews with millennials and the multiple *Millennial Impact Reports* that social justice and equity is a critical component of this generation (Millennial Impact Report 2015, 2016, *Ten Years Looking Back*). Each generation has responded to social justice but with different names. The Great Depression created a multitude of nonprofits in the 1930s and World War II that involved women with many of the young men away at war. The Civil Rights Movement came in the 60s. Black Lives Matter on the backdrop of COVID-19 also created its own justice movement that many millennials engaged in for social equity.

Additionally, millennial donors look to the cause and not the institution, so nonprofits will have to market themselves appropriately. Aligning with a cause creates a sense of equity. Unfortunately for many institutions that have spent decades building brands, this branding no longer matters to millennials (unless the organization is tarnished). In other words, the organizations need to foreground their mission and not emphasize the institution. Nonprofits' messaging and fundraising opportunities should provide a reframing of their work. For example, a hospital may look at how their important work provides access to the underserved and a higher education institution is lifting someone out of poverty by providing educational opportunities. This reframing of messaging creates a social justice lens and pinpoints funding opportunities. In other words, nonprofits need to be their authentic selves (despite millennials' need for the perfect social media filter!) (Fig. 7.2).

Fundraising events are pivoting as well. From the interviews and studies we have looked at, nonprofits need to acknowledge that large, expensive events are not desirable for this generation. Millennials still want to engage face-to-face instead of just buying a plate of rubber chicken to show their support or only being engaged online (though that is still important). Nonprofits will, therefore, need to develop other fundraising activities that are more attractive (and more cost-effective and transparent) to millennials. Events need to come across as genuine and about the mission. They want a seat at the table when it comes to helping nonprofits, but happily they will bring their friends if you give them access. Of course bringing their friends means that they also see volunteering as an opportunity to network (for friends, work, and even romance). Unlike previous generations, this generation connects everything together just like their lives online.

The intersectionality of work, socialization, and philanthropy is very evident with the millennial generation. They look at philanthropy as an opportunity to engage in all three. No longer is giving done in silos. Millennials now expect nonprofits they support through volunteerism and

Fig. 7.2 GRACE Gala (Photo Credit: GRACE)

donations to be a place to professionally network as well and engage in supporting a cause as a changemaker as well. As we reflect back at the case study of BvB, the members really wanted to be part of making a change and felt they could impact a global issue with Alzheimer's locally.

I want to end with three broad suggestions on how to best engage with potential millennial donors. First, nonprofits have opportunities to engage with millennials through social network engagement. Second, millennials have shifted the way they engage with fundraising events from the day of large-scale galas to feet on the ground, friend-engaging events and utilizing social media interaction. Finally, millennials also have a deep engagement with technology that continues to shift over time. By examining these areas, the nonprofit community can begin to learn how to better envision ways to engage the millennial population for volunteerism and philanthropy.

Extend Their Networks

Nonprofits need to tap into and feed the networks of millennials. Sometimes a millennial engages in a philanthropic cause that is social and sometimes participants get involved to "support a friend" even if the cause becomes his or her cause. The dual purpose provides a window into the kinds of engagement in social networks that millennials crave. Millennials come to nonprofits with more than an idea or cause in mind. We are seeing this even with the next generation (like Paper for Water). They will bring their social networks as well. For our youth, they come with a cause in mind because they saw it on social media or the internet. Lean in and be okay with serving a purpose and support their networks through more than just an event—through boards, groups, and committees. Face-to-face still is important, overlaid with technology, transparency, and friend connections. By engaging them like a million-dollar donor now, you will see the long-term value later. And in some circumstances, you will see major gifts and leadership gifts and the beginnings of planned gifts and amazing volunteerism. But always remember this cohort's background and the catered messaging they are used to. As the Great Transfer Wealth has begun and the millennial generation earns its own money, nonprofits need to prepare to be on their list of preferred nonprofits for philanthropy and volunteerism.

Shake Up Your Fundraising Events

Fundraising events often serve as the anchor for annual revenue for nonprofits including galas, luncheons, receptions, lectures, home tours, parades, comedy events, music events, and plays. These events connect the public to the mission of the nonprofit, but not all speak to the interests of millennials. The diversity of events that BvB Dallas offers—Words with Friends, an eSports event, a golf tournament, and an in-person football game—exemplifies the way today's nonprofits have to reach millennials and Generation Z. Some BvB Dallas members even create fundraising events for their individual fundraising goals, hosting parties for the cause or other creative events to reach their fundraising goals. We saw this with GRACE and their places of worship and Paper for Water and their corporate partnerships and youth volunteers. And let us not forget that these millennials and Generation Z give themselves. Be prepared to let them take leadership and hear their ideas. The next generations know how to connect and connect wide.

Utilize Social Media to Its Fullest Potential

Millennials as digital natives grew up in an era of technology which enables them to use it with ease. As the literature has shown, millennials utilize Facebook, but millennials also report using GroupMe, YouTube, Instagram,

LinkedIn, and Pinterest (with more limited use of Twitter and Snapchat). Recently emerging platforms that millennials are now using more regularly include Parler, TikTok, WeChat, Tumblr, Be Real, and Reddit. To address the need to reach millennials, BvB Dallas recently purchased CRM software, allowing them to organize their email exchanges, accounting, and even their social media handles. BvB Dallas has a communications committee that maintains a regular online presence and members are encouraged to engage with posts. They also use the giving platforms as an outlet for giving, for donors to send well-wishes, and to solicit donations. The particular giving platforms used by BvB created a sense of community and an opportunity to engage with friends, family, and co-workers. GRACE has integrated software that tracks volunteerism and philanthropy and multiple social media platforms to engage all generations. Paper for Water has had extreme success across media which enables them to continue to have "something shareable" and they shifted to virtual events during the pandemic. However, participants in the studies we've looked at still noted that social media was only one tool in fundraising. The majority still had the personal connection as their number one source of fundraising, including in-person and online from friends, family, and co-workers.

Finally, all three of these recommendations—using and extending millennial networks, offering creative events and social media platforms—also help nonprofits to "cut through the noise" of the number of nonprofits competing with one another to create genuine millennial engagement. And that's what we're ultimately after!

The roadmap that follows this chapter is a guidepost for you and your nonprofit. Each is individualized based on size, location, age of organization, health, and willingness to work with the next generation, and so no checklist could be one-size-fits-all. But it can put a spotlight on millennial philanthropy—something near and dear to my heart, and I hope for you too.

Best wishes—now go enjoy a latte and avocado toast!

Millennial Engagement

A Roadmap

Communications

What social media channels are you on?
Is it smartphone friendly?
Do the millennials "see" themselves in your communications?
Is the engagement genuine?
Do you have something shareable (brand ambassadors, etc.)?
Do they feel like they are part of something good?

Volunteer

Are millennials asked to be on your committees or boards?
When engaged, do they have a seat at your table?
Are they being asked for meaningful donations?

Brand Awareness

Does your organization share an avenue on how they make a difference (no matter its size)?
Can you explain your impact (even if the issue is larger/global issue)?

Events

Are the events genuine?
Do you have transparency what the funds will go towards?
Will your events make an impact?
Do you have diversity in your events (style, format)?

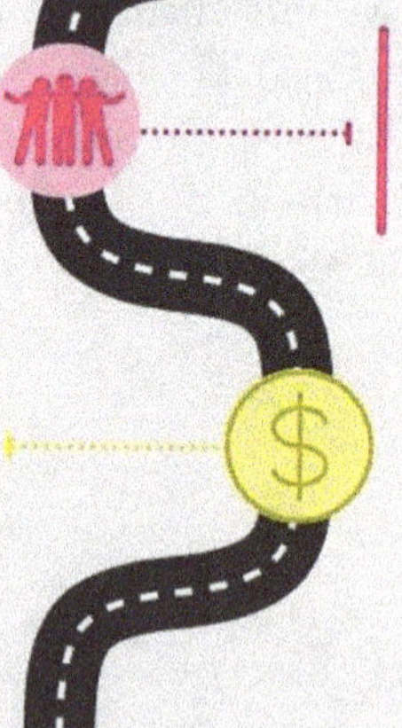

Network

Do you have engagement that can include their social networks?
Do they have opportunities to socialize?

Donations

Do you have online and in-person options?
Can the person designate their gift?
How do you communicate making an impact with a social justice lens?

References

Kelly, Jack. 2019. "Millennials Will Become Richest Generation In American History As Baby Boomers Transfer Over Their Wealth." Accessed November 1, 2019. https://www.forbes.com/sites/jackkelly/2019/10/26/millennials-will-become-richest-generation-in-american-history-as-baby-boomers-transfer-over-their-wealth/?sh=3cb879f76c4b.

Levitz, Eric. 2021. "Will 'the Great Wealth Transfer' Trigger a Millennial Civil War?" Accessed November 1, 2019. https://nymag.com/intelligencer/2021/07/will-the-great-wealth-transfer-spark-a-millennial-civil-war.html.

Millennial Impact Report. 2015. Accessed May 30, 2017. http://www.themillennialimpact.com/past-research.

Millennial Impact Report. 2016. Accessed May 30, 2017. http://www.themillennialimpact.com/past-research.

"Millennial Impact Report: 10 Years Looking Back." 2020. Accessed May 30, 2017. http://www.themillennialimpact.com/latest-research.

Index

H. Hull Miori, *Millennial Philanthropy*,
https://doi.org/10.1007/978-3-031-30269-5

Printed in the USA
CPSIA information can be obtained
at www.ICGtesting.com
CBHW070440080524
8181CB00006BA/275